Distinctively Presbyterian

Distinctively Presbyterian

William E. Chapman

Witherspoon
PRESS

Louisville, Kentucky

Publisher: *Sandra Albritton Moak*
Editor: *Martha Schull Gilliss*
Book interior: *Carol E. Johnson*

First edition
Published by Witherspoon Press
Louisville, Kentucky

Web site address: www.pcusa.org/witherspoon

PRINTED IN THE UNITED STATES OF AMERICA
06 07 08 09 10 11 12 14 15 16—10 9 8 7 6 5 4 3 2 1

Library of Congress Cataloging-in-Publication Data

Chapman, William E., 1933-
  Distinctively Presbyterian / William E. Chapman ; Martha Gilliss, editor. --
1st ed.
    p. cm.
  Includes bibliographical references.
  ISBN 1-57153-060-6 (pbk. : alk. paper)
1. Presbyterian Church (U.S.A.) Book of order. 2. Presbyterian Church
(U.S.A.)--Government. I. Gilliss, Martha S. II. Title.
  BX8969.6.C44 2006
  285'.137--dc22
                                   2006013371

Contents

Foreword

This project is the fruit of two invitations. One was the encouragement of Stated Clerk Clifton Kirkpatrick to write another book dealing with one of the first four chapters of the *Book of Order*. The other was an invitation from Rev. Ann Clifton to lead an officer-training event for the East Dallas Cluster in Grace Presbytery on November 20, 2004. The result is this manuscript.

It is not uncommon for writers, such as Edward Mains and Jumpa Lahiri, to begin their novels through the voice of someone else telling a story. Perhaps if we read the *Book of Order* as the story of how some people over the years have tried to give shape to God's call to be faithful together, we could hear the testimony of those who have gone before us, rather than chafing against specific provisions contrary to our personal tastes. My earlier books have also shared what I hear when I ponder the *Book of Order*.

The title seems pretentious at first glance. It comes from the nine "Principles of Presbyterian Government" in G-4.0301 in our *Book of Order*. Discussing these with experienced church officers seldom generates many comments, other than surprise that they are written down. My hope is that this book will enable newly elected officers to appreciate how the Presbyterian Church (U.S.A.) goes about its witness to the gospel of Jesus Christ, the head of the church.

As always, I must thank several persons whose encouragement and patience provided continuing support for this project. An invitation from Rev. Ann Clifton to the East Dallas Cluster in Grace Presbytery for its training event November 20, 2004, titled "Picture and Frame," was an opportunity to scout out the topic with church officers from another region of the country than my own. A major learning from that event was how deeply in the psyche of experienced church officers the "Principles of Presbyterian Government" are. Dialogue with this group served to focus the topic and encourage me in this endeavor.

As with my previous publications, Elder Clifford Sherrod of Grace Presbyterian Church, Midland, Texas, has patiently provided encouragement as well as an elder's perspective as the chapters emerged. I am continually sustained spiritually by the worship in the Ridgewood, West Side Presbyterian Church, and by colleagues in ministry there and across our denomination. The encouragement of Rev. Clifton Kirkpatrick, Stated Clerk of the General Assembly and his colleague Rev. Mark Tammen are artesian wells of refreshment for me.

My wife Zitta and the rest of the family help in numerous ways. Zitta continues to keep my sentences well formed before others see them.

I am deeply thankful to God for all the people and experiences that come together as I work to provide resources for officers of the Presbyterian Church (U.S.A.).

Four Presbyterian Characteristics: My Reflections

W hat is distinctive about Presbyterians? Dirk Wierenga chose a combination of text and words in *Presbyterians: A Spiritual Journey* to answer this question. He began by interviewing Presbyterians as he traveled across the country. Later he sent photographers to illustrate what he had found. He organized his book into three chapters: "Stories of Faith," "Spiritual Communities," and "Connectional Bodies." The first chapter is about individuals, the second is about specific congregations and their mission; and the last deals with the larger church.[1]

Wierenga joins numerous others from many perspectives who have provided answers to this question over the years. Books, periodicals, and web sites have emerged in the last fifty years espousing what it means to be distinctively Presbyterian. I join this chorus and add yet another personal testimony for consideration and discussion.

In this book, I will consider chapter IV of the *Book of Order,* which includes a section called "Principles of Presbyterian Government" (G-4.0300). Chapter I bears the title, "Preliminary Principles," basic understandings drawn from our heritage. Among the sections are "The Historic Principles of Church Order" (G-1.0300) and "The Historic Principles of Church Government" (G-1.0400).

My contention is that chapter IV addresses the issue of what holds the Presbyterian Church (U.S.A.) together. The reunion of 1983, which reunited two Presbyterian denominations that had been separated since1861, resulted in a major revision of the *Book of Order*.[2] This book deals with this historical development in a later chapter.

At this stage, I present four characteristics of Presbyterians I have known from various areas of the country—people with varying degrees of responsibility and diverse theological and social perspectives. These folks share an ongoing commitment to and comfort with the Presbyterian way of being church. Those who find these qualities strange or wrong are invited to challenge them.

The four aspects of life in the Presbyterian Church that connects these persons all begin with the letter "d." They are: dilemma, dialogue, debate, and deference.

Dilemma

The first aspect of being Presbyterian is comfort with **dilemma**. Presbyterians tend to be suspicious of simple answers. A dilemma is a difficult decision, in which the need for decision is urgent while the options are nearly equal in either a positive or negative way. A dilemma arises from a paradox, defined as a "a seemingly absurd or self-contradictory statement or proposition which when investigated or explained may prove to be well-founded or true."[3] Some, understanding that life is perplexing, would call this awareness of paradox realism. A situation of paradox can be created when both sides of a controversy find validity with their perspective. Op-ed columnist David Brooks, in a piece about theologian John Stott, wrote the following:

> There's been a lot of twaddle written recently about the supposed opposition between faith and reason. To read Stott is to see someone practicing "thoughtful allegiance" to scripture. For him, Christianity means probing the mysteries of Christ. He is always exploring paradoxes. Jesus teaches humility, so why does he talk about himself so much? What does it mean to gain power through weakness, or freedom through obedience? In many cases the truth is not found in the middle of apparent opposites, but on both extremes simultaneously.[4]

Neither Stott nor Brooks are Presbyterians, as far as I know. What Brooks offers is the clearest, most succinct description of paradox I have seen.

Dilemmas are the stuff of life. While we Americans celebrate the freedom to choose, we also appreciate that contemporary life often produces difficult, even painful choices. For example, advances in medical care mean that we now confront choices and challenges beyond our comprehension or preparation, such as

determining whether and when to remove life support for someone we love.

The central paradox of the Christian faith is the teaching that,
as John's gospel puts it, "The Word became flesh and lived
among us . . ." (John 1:14). How can it be that God becomes
human? This divine paradox stands at the core of our faith, one
that continues to trouble many, even after centuries of theological
debate. Those few words of John challenge our assumptions
about who God is and what we mean when we speak of God.
Charles Wesley wrote,

> Veiled in flesh, the Godhead see;
> Hail the incarnate Deity,
> Pleased in flesh with us to dwell,
> Jesus, our Emmanuel.[5]

This is more than poetry set to music. It is, rather, a succinct
affirmation of the central mystery of the Christian faith.

I submit that a benefit of recognizing a dilemma is the opportunity to revisit previous resolutions of continuing tensions in
church life and to adjust the resolution in the light of fresh understandings and new insights. At the heart of our fellowship is an
awareness that "time makes ancient good uncouth."[6] The
unavoidable challenge before us is to distinguish the issues behind
the dilemmas and those that reflect the core of our faith. "[W]e
have this treasure in clay jars," wrote the Apostle Paul (2 Cor. 4:7).

Paul also wrote about the "varieties of gifts" (1 Cor. 12:4ff, Eph.
4:11–13, Rom. 12:6–7). Discerning these gifts is yet another requirement of faithfulness to "the whole counsel of God."[7] In a time when
many impatiently dismiss complexity as too troubling, the challenge Presbyterians face is to continue to witness to the good news
as offering strength to work through dilemmas to fresh insights.

Dilemmas or paradoxes are triggers for temptation, when one
asks, "Should I or shouldn't I?" Dilemmas are perilous, as to
some degree are all our choices, all our decisions. Some work out
well. Others don't. Every choice has a cost, which sooner or later
must be paid. Part of the cost is living with the way our choices
turn out and then determining what we will do next. That is life,
both inside and outside the church. The difference is that in the
church we learn about forgiveness and new life.

Many Presbyterians have what psychologists call "tolerance for ambiguity." This awareness of the complex issues of life contributes to a healthy humility, one that affirms convictions boldly and makes one willing to discuss the issues directly and skillfully, all the while understanding that a group decision is more likely to be more correct than an individual one. I have often found that my initial reaction to some actions of various Presbyterian entities has been negative, only later to discover that the decision made was more productive in the long run than I would have thought.

The "Preliminary Principles," a document drafted at the same time as the "Constitution of the United States of America," affirms eight principles of church order (G-1.0300), which present complex issues of life together in a community of faith.[8] In 1797 the General Assembly articulated what we now call "The Historic Principles of Church Order," proclaiming "that a majority shall govern . . ." (G-1.0400). This affirmation of democracy in the life of the church has major implications, which will emerge as we walk together on this quest to determine what is distinctive about Presbyterians.

Accepting the church as God's gift to us, the body of Christ, Presbyterians understand that we are "bound to his authority and thus free to live in the lively, joyous reality of the grace of God" (G-1.0100d). Such a statement thrusts us into the paradox of being bound yet free, forgiven sinners.

Dialogue

A second aspect of being Presbyterian is a commitment to **dialogue**. To listen to God as Creator and Lord includes listening carefully to brothers and sisters through whom God's Spirit often speaks. This last statement indicates a point at which there has been, and continues to be, serious difference among Presbyterians. It has historically been a challenge, one that has troubled Presbyterians, as well as other Christians and Jews, throughout history.

We see similarly diverging viewpoints in the Hebrew Bible around the issue of relating the Five Books of Moses and the Books of the Prophets. We see evidence of this ongoing tension in the New Testament in the dispute between the Pharisees and Sadducees. The question boils down to how the Ten Commandments were to be understood in the life of the covenant community of

Israel. How were the provisions from Mount Sinai to be understood as Israel's life situation changed?

The New Testament suggests that political situations further complicated this religious dispute. The writer of the Qumran cave manuscripts rails against "'seekers after smooth things,'" who could well be Pharisees.[9] Anthony J. Saldarini summarizes his view of such groups as follows:

> The Pharisaic association probably functioned as a social movement organization seeking to change society. The social, political, and economic situation of Palestinian Jews underwent a number of upheavals in the Greco-Roman period which demanded adaptation of Jewish customs and a reinterpretation of the Jewish identity fashioned by the biblical tradition. The Hasmoneans and the governing class changed Israel into a small, militarily active Hellenistic kingdom and took control of political and economic resources in order to control society. The Pharisees probably sought a new, communal commitment to a strict Jewish way of life based on adherence to the covenant.[10]

Saldarini's quote sheds light on the dynamics we find in Jesus' response to the question of John's disciples about fasting (Matt. 9:14). Putting a new patch on old cloth when the old is no longer functional only makes matters worse. Similarly, putting new, still-fermenting wine into a wineskin wrinkled with age means that both wine and container will be lost. The dilemma is determining when the new wine is worth conserving before time has passed.

When we Presbyterians have found ourselves facing a dilemma, at our best, we have sought to achieve resolution with dialogue. Describing such a process, G-1.0100c in the *Book of Order* states, "matters are to be ordered according to the Word by reason and sound judgment, under the guidance of the Holy Spirit."[11] The meanings and interrelationships of four terms—Word, reason, sound judgment, and Holy Spirit—are open to interpretation. As a whole, they illustrate a necessary, yet complex, dialogical process for determining the details of life together in a Presbyterian community. Each of these has served as a focus of Presbyterian disputes, alerting us to the need to be especially sensitive to the volatile nature of these aspects of our life together.

Much turn-of-the-millennium American controversy in both political and church circles has a focus on reason. What is usually termed "concern for principles" seems to me to be more accurately a quest for authority derived from principles or rules. I find it curious that much of the rhetoric from both ends of the political and ecclesiastical spectrums is their agreement that principles are essential. The popular way to describe the differences among them is to use labels such as "conservative" or "liberal," or even "left" and "right," as shorthand for the complex issues involved. Rather than discussing our differences, we base our correctness on a particular principle or set of principles that we assume to be more correct than those of the other side. Commitment to principle often leads to acrimony between adherents of the two positions.

Reason has a close comrade in this list: sound judgment. A phrase in the Westminster Confession, "a due use of the ordinary means," used in reference to things that are necessary for salvation (6.007), describes this phenomenon. Today we might call it common sense.

The Presbyterian commitment to rationality can be traced to John Calvin, whose *Institutes of the Christian Religion* and his commentaries on Scripture reveal a tough-minded believer wrestling with presenting his faith in Jesus Christ as eminently reasonable. Calvin's intent was educational:

> Moreover, it has been my purpose in this labor to prepare and instruct candidates in sacred theology for the reading of the divine Word, in order that they may be able both to have easy access to it and to advance in it without stumbling. For I believe I have so embraced the sum of religion in all its parts, and have arranged it in such an order, that if anyone rightly grasps it, it will not be difficult for him to determine what he ought especially to seek in Scripture, and to what end he ought to relate its contents.[12]

Calvin appeals to both heart and head as he organizes his understanding of the Christian faith.

The Scots Confession, ratified in 1560, demonstrates how John Knox translated Calvin's reasonable approach to Christian faith from a Reformed perspective into a confession of faith for the Church of Scotland. The Westminster Confession was an attempt of Presbyterians in England to explain their faith in a reasoned way. One hundred fifty-one persons worked from 1643 to

1649 to produce the confession and two catechisms.[13] Adopted by American Presbyterians in 1729, these "Westminster Standards" continue to guide us. The adoption of the Confession of 1967 and A Brief Statement of Faith in 1991, as well as other historical confessional documents, provide rich evidence of how our Reformed heritage has continued to adapt to new situations.

The Book of Confessions is considered to be Part I of *The Constitution of the Presbyterian Church (U.S.A.)* (G-1.0500). Elders and ministers vow in their ordination and installation to "receive and adopt the essential tenets of the Reformed faith as expressed in the confessions of our church as authentic and reliable expositions of what Scripture leads us to believe and do . . ." (G-14.0207c and G-14.0405b(3)). These confessions are the lens through which Presbyterians examine Scripture, and they have developed over centuries of reflection and discussion regarding what constitutes Christian faith from a particular perspective.

When the United Presbyterian Church in the United States of America adopted *The Book of Confessions* in 1967, major opposition arose by those who felt that the Westminster Confession continued to be sufficient for church life. It has been interesting to note how those who were so vigorous in their opposition to *The Book of Confessions*, now seem to have forgotten that the Westminster Confessions is still in force. For example, Westminster's extensive discussion of the authority of Scripture includes guidance that recourse is to be to the "whole counsel of God . . . [which] is either expressly set down in Scripture, or . . . may be deduced from Scripture." In addition, "there are some circumstances concerning the worship of God and government of the Church, common to human actions and societies, which are to be ordered by the light of nature and Christian prudence, according to the general rules of the Word, which are always to be observed."[14] Again, reasoned discussion finds a place in our Presbyterian process dating back to the mid-seventeenth century.

The Bible, which is expressed in the Westminster Confession as "Word," continues to be for Presbyterians the "unique and authoritative witness" to the good news of Jesus Christ, the ultimate criterion of faith and practice (G-14.0207b and G-14.0405b(2)). The discovery of a specific scriptural instance of support for a certain practice is insufficient warrant for adopting that provision. Presbyterian practice is at its best when it carefully explores the "whole counsel of God's word" prior to adopting some practice for church life—or excising it.

The goal for Presbyterian dialogue is not to win but to discover that God is calling us, individually and collectively, to faithful membership, as we shall see when we consider G-4.0300d. At this point the final characteristic, Holy Spirit, enters the discussion. As we will see further, Presbyterians understand the role of the Holy Spirit to be evident in community process, rather than in personal assertion.[15]

Debate

The third aspect of being Presbyterian is willingness to **debate**. The difference between dialogue and **debate** is subtle, yet significant. Dialogue involves discussion; conversation, exploration, and consideration are aspects of its dynamics. **Debate** is a formally prepared process of interchange, the result of which is determined by a third party. The difference is the degree of stress placed on those making the decision. The intent of debate is to fashion a useful resolution of the dilemma, the best resolution that those responsible are capable of making.

"Come now, let us argue it out, says the LORD . . ." (Isa. 1:18). "Argue it out" has replaced "reason together," which is found in older versions of the text. The more recent version may strike us as confrontational. Perhaps this is because we have forgotten that debate is supposed to be a civilized quest for resolution of disputes. Living in a sound-byte culture where media encourages alternate points of view—but only as long as they are limited to less than two or three minutes—means that patient, productive debate is increasingly difficult.

A further cultural factor is the emergence of confrontational advocacy. Americans have learned that zeal expressed through emotionally charged language is an effective device for a small group to get attention for their cause or perspective. "Staying on message" is the contemporary motto of advocacy. Stalwart repetition of claims has mostly replaced thoughtful exchange and reasoned discussion. "Attack ads" are generally acceptable and often supported by those who agree with their content. The casualty of these stratagems is the health of the community, no matter if this is a civil or ecclesiastical issue.

Recent experience in Presbyterian governing bodies suggests that the cultural patterns of interaction have invaded all public discourse. I find it almost amusing that those who are most earnest about traditional values have been quick to adopt these newer forms of advocacy. Commissioners in governing bodies rise with prepared speeches, written before the discussion has begun, to espouse their point of view, rather than seeking through debate or discussion to arrive at a reasonable resolution of whatever issue is being considered.

What seems to have been lost is the understanding that dialogue and debate are not about winning but about joining together in a quest for faithful discipleship. On a quest such as this, one more understood rule should prevail. Debate is a quest for truth, with awareness that what I understand to be a correct response in a given situation needs the contribution of my colleagues from a different perspective if it is to have the rigor necessary for coping with the complexities of life.

Deference

The fourth aspect of being Presbyterian is **deference**, which is also called civility, and in the language of the Bible, humility. For Presbyterians, deference is related to the doctrine of God's sovereignty. The *Book of Order* indicates that this doctrine affirms "the majesty, holiness, and providence of God who creates, sustains, rules, and redeems the world in the freedom of sovereign righteousness and love" (G-2.0500a). God is great in the way that God redeems and gives hope and energy to humankind, reminding us that we are only human. As Paul wrote to the Romans, "O the depth of the riches and wisdom and knowledge of God! How unsearchable are his judgements and how inscrutable his ways!" (Rom. 11:33–34).

The majesty of the Creator inspires awe and humility in creatures. Appreciation of God's greatness is intensified by the wonder of God's forgiving love in Jesus Christ and the regular public confession of sin. The *Book of Common Worship* describes this aspect of worship as follows:

> In words of scripture the people are called to confess the reality of sin in personal and common life. Claiming the promises of God sealed in our baptism, we humbly confess our sin. . . .

Having confessed our sin, we remember the promises of God's redemption, and the claims God has on all human life. The assurance of God's forgiving grace is declared in the name of Jesus Christ. We accept God's forgiveness, confident that in dying to sin, God raises us to new life.[16]

Notice that confession is for corporate as well as personal sin. Deference to one another in church life witnesses to awareness that each of us needs the others in the community of faith to enable us to grow in our discipleship. The following demonstrates how a prayer of confession provides the basis for community:

O Lord our God, you know who we are: men and women, girls and boys with good consciences and with bad; people who are content and those who are discontented; the certain and the uncertain; Christians by conviction and Christians by convention; those who believe, those who half believe, and those who disbelieve.

We now stand before you, in all out differences, yet alike in that we are all in the wrong with you and with one another.

Forgive us, cleanse us, renew us, unite us, redirect us by your grace promised to us and to all in Jesus Christ our Lord.[17]

We need one another as we seek to act in ways that are worthy of our calling. Such regular confession and assurance remind Presbyterians where we fit in the scheme of God's creation. God's gifts to people vary, and so we need to hear one another as we seek to live faithful lives.

The roots of this understanding of the human need for community reach back to Genesis 2, where God comments, 'It is not good for the human to be alone, I shall make a sustainer beside him.'[18] Subsequently, a people comes into being, eventually receiving a covenant as the abiding foundation for community. We Presbyterians see ourselves as connected by a covenant, as described in the *Book of Order*:

The law and government of the Presbyterian Church (U.S.A.) presuppose the fellowship of women and men with their children in voluntary covenanted relationship with one another and with God through Jesus Christ. The organization rests upon the fellowship and is not designed to work without trust and love. (G-7.0103)

Civility is essential to the health of a covenant community. Presbyterian history has not always exemplified deference or civility as we have sought to be faithful. The first schism between American Presbyterians arose in 1741. Led by Gilbert Tennent, the issue at stake was to determine whether or not the good news was being properly preached. The division into Old Side and New Side remained until 1758, when Tennent was elected moderator of the reunited synod. This was nine years after he had decided that the division was unfortunate and should be ended.[19] There have been subsequent divisions and reconciliations throughout Presbyterian history in America. The tension between zeal on the one hand and civility on the other continues to trouble our fellowship as we look toward the Presbyterian tercentennial in 2010.

This concludes my reflections on what I propose to be four important personal characteristics of Presbyterians. My ministry has connected me with Presbyterians across the United States. It has been a privilege for me to be a member of six presbyteries.[20] This discussion also builds on my four years as a member of the General Assembly Council, the most carefully crafted diverse group of Presbyterians of which I have ever been a part. I recognize that appreciation for the four aspects I have discussed is rarely exemplified in one particular Presbyterian. Yet I feel that there is merit in suggesting that these are aspects that, if put into practice, would enable our fellowship to be a more effective witness to the gospel we profess.

Notes

1. Dick Wierenga, *Presbyterians: A Spiritual Journey* (Louisville: Geneva Press, 2000),
2. An earlier division, between the Old School and the New School in 1837–1838 was complicated by the Civil War.
3. "Paradox," *Shorter Oxford English Dictionary on Historical Principles*, 5th ed., vol. 2 (Oxford, UK: Oxford University Press), p. 2092.
4. David Brooks, "Who Is John Stott" *New York Times*, 30 November 2004, sec. A p. 28.
5. "Hark! The Herald Angels Sing," *The Presbyterian Hymnal* (Louisville: Westminster/John Knox Press, 1990), no. 31.

6. James Russell Lowell, "The Kingdom of God on Earth," in *The Hymnal* (Philadelphia: Presbyterian Board of Christian Education, 1933) no. 373.
7. The Westminster Confession of Faith, *The Book of Confessions: Study Edition. Part 1 of the Constitution of the Presbyterian Church (U.S.A)* (Louisville: Geneva Press, 1996), 6.006.
8. For a discussion of these, see my *History and Theology in the Book of Order: Blood on Every Page* (Louisville: Witherspoon Press, 1999).
9. Anthony J. Saldarini, "Pharisees," Vol. 5 of *The Anchor Bible Dictionary*, ed. David Noel Freedman (New York: Doubleday, 1992), p. 301.
10. Ibid., p. 302.
11. I named this clause a "quadrate formula" and reflected on its implications in Chapman, *Finding Christ in the Book of Order* (Louisville: Witherspoon Press, 2003), pp. 63–66.
12. *Calvin: Institutes of the Christian Religion*, vol. XX, of *The Library of Christian Classics*, ed. John T. McNeil, trans. Ford Lewis Battle (Philadelphia: The Westminster Press, 1960), p. 4.
13. *Book of Confessions: Study Edition, Part 1 of the Constitution of the Presbyterian Church (U.S.A)* (Louisville: Geneva Press), pp. 162–165.
14. The Westminster Confession of Faith, *The Book of Confessions*, 6.006.
15. For another treatment of these four qualities, see my *Finding Christ in the Book of Order* (Louisville: Witherspoon Press, 2003), pp. 61–65.
16. *Book of Common Worship*, ed. The Theology and Worship Ministry Unit (Louisville: Westminster/John Knox Press, 1993), p. 35.
17. Church bulletin, West Side Presbyterian Church, Ridgewood, NJ, January 30, 2005, p. 2.
18. Robert Alter, *The Five Books of Moses: A Translation with Commentary* (New York: W. W. Norton & Company, 2004), pp. 21–22.
19. See Milton J. Coalter, Jr., *Gilbert Tennet, Son of Thunder: A Case Study of Pietism's Impact on the First Great Awakening in the Middle Colonies.* A publication of the Presbyterian Historical Society (Westport: Greenwood Press, Inc., 1986).
20. In order, the presbyteries of Omaha, Winnebago, Monmouth, Washington City, Philadelphia, Palo Duro Union, and Palisades. Three of these names are no longer used. Omaha is now Missouri River Valley; Palo Duro Union is Palo Duro, and Washington City is now National Capital. I was a candidate under both Lansing (now Lake Michigan) and Philadelphia presbyteries.

G-4.0101

The Church universal consists of all persons in every nation, together with their children, who profess faith in Jesus Christ as Lord and Savior and commit themselves to live in a fellowship under his rule.

G-4.0103

A particular church consists of those persons in a particular place, along with their children, who profess faith in Jesus Christ as Lord and Savior and who have been gathered for the service of God as set forth in Scripture, subject to a particular form of church government.

ONE

The Church— Universal and Particular

I

G-4.0101

"The Church universal consists of all persons in every nation, together with their children, who profess faith in Jesus Christ as Lord and Savior and commit themselves to live in a fellowship under his rule." "Distinctively Presbyterian" is a phrase that can be understood in a number of ways. The sentence above sets the breathtaking context of the church universal. The phrase "All persons in every nation" goes far beyond the Presbyterian tradition. What a curious way to begin a discussion of distinctiveness!

The point is to remind Presbyterians that we understand ourselves to be part of Christian history. Such an affirmation reminds us that we are neither exclusivist nor dismissive of other traditions. The basis for this statement is found in the first three chapters of the *Book of Order*. Chapter I (G-1.0000) discusses "church" in two sections before mentioning "the Presbyterian Church (U.S.A.)" in G-1.0300. Chapter II, "The Church and Its Confessions" (G-2.0000), only arrives at our "expression of the Reformed tradition" in G-2.0500 after outlining how all this connects with historic Christian doctrines. The name of our denomination never appears in Chapter III (G-3.0000) "The Church and Its Mission."

The phrase "together with their children," follows "all persons in every nation" and echoes Jesus' command, "Let the little children come to me" (Matt. 19:14, Mark 10:14, Luke 18:16) and extends the definition of church to include all generations. Such realism about passing on the faith to our children is the root of the Presbyterian tradition of education. The scriptural basis for this is Acts 2:39: "For the promise is for you, for your children, and for all who are far away, everyone whom the Lord our God calls to him."

A minister in the Church of Christ, responding to my question of how that denomination came into being, replied, "The first members were Presbyterians who no longer knew how to read!" Yet Christian education seems to be increasingly peripheral to our understanding of mission. Focus on the number of members and preoccupation with the level of giving have been at the expense of teaching our members the Bible and our heritage and endangers our continuing vitality as a denomination.

One of the verbs at the heart of G-4.0101 is "profess," a choice that is significant. The *Shorter Oxford English Dictionary* defines "profess" as a transitive verb, a verb with an object. It means to "Affirm or declare one's faith in or allegiance to (a religion, principle, action, etc.)." (definition 4).[1] The public nature of the declaration also comes from the Latin root for this word. Chapter V of the *Book of Order* clarifies that admission to membership in the Presbyterian Church (U.S.A.) involves both baptism and a public profession of faith (G-5.0101). When one makes a statement regarding one's faith in public, such a declaration is to be taken seriously. Of course, people can make such statements unwisely or frivolously. Even so, the presumption of the seriousness of one's profession is essential for a community of faith.

This understanding of church as a community of faith comes from the Westminster Confession of Faith: "The visible Church, which is also catholic or universal under the gospel (not confined to one nation as before under the law), consists of all those throughout the world that profess the true religion, together with their children." (6.141).[2] According to a footnote in the *Book of Confessions,* the original text of Westminster (1647) read simply "and their children."[3] While this seems a slight change, the substitution of "together with" for "and" stresses more appropriately the relational and connective quality of the church and refers directly back to the preceding paragraph in the Westminster Confession: "The catholic or universal church which is invisible, consists of the whole number of the elect, that have been, are, or shall be gathered into one, under Christ the head thereof;

and is the spouse, the body, the fullness of Him that filleth all in all" (6.140).[4]

Beyond the churches we know and see is yet another church, traditionally called the communion of saints.[5] Westminster teaches that this is the pure church, which, because of its purity, is beyond human knowing. Only God has knowledge of the perfect church and the roll of members. Yearn as we may to be part of such a church, it is beyond human ability to ascertain its membership. This provision also suggests that churches claiming to be pure are making claims they cannot support.

The Westminster Confession has provided a distinctively Presbyterian understanding of the church for American Presbyterians since colonial times. Noting that it is to the visible or catholic[6] church that ministry and sacraments are given, it goes on to assert realistically that "[t]he purest churches under heaven are subject both to mixture and error. . . . Nevertheless, there shall be always a Church on earth, to worship God according to his will" (6.144).[7]

An earlier example of theological realism emerges in Chapter XVIII of the Scots Confession (1560). Chapter XVIII is titled, "The Notes by Which the True Kirk Shall Be Determined from the False, and Who Shall Be Judge of Doctrine." It states the criteria for a true church:

> The notes of the true Kirk, therefore, we believe, confess and avow to be:
>   first, the true preaching of the Word of God, in which God has revealed himself to us, as the writings of the prophets and apostles declare;
>   secondly, the right administration of the sacraments of Christ Jesus, with which must be associated the Word and promise of God to seal and confirm them in our hearts; and
>   lastly, ecclesiastical discipline rightly administered, as God's Word prescribes, whereby vice is repressed and virtue nourished.[8]

These three criteria marking a congregation as a true church represent a challenge inasmuch as they name the responsibility surrounding the communication and sharing of God's Word. The final statement of Chapter XVIII indicates the delicacy of this work: "We dare not receive or admit any interpretation which is contrary to any principal point of our faith, or to any other plain text of Scripture, or to the rule of love."[9]

These confessional statements present a theological realism that is deeply rooted in Presbyterian history. Such realism argues for some humility regarding the way we approach our discipleship. Presbyterians believe deeply and seriously, yet with humility, and are willing to discuss and explore their beliefs. The initial understanding of church as it appears in these confessions and as is clarified in the *Book of Order* provides the basis for cooperation with other Christian bodies.

Since 2003, the historic practice of providing "scriptural allusions" for the *Book of Order* was resumed, after having been suspended for several decades.[10] The term "scriptural allusion" was chosen over two other traditional terms. "Proof texting" was a practice of the Westminster Assembly that was insisted on by Parliament as a way to demonstrate that there was some biblical basis for various provisions.[11] The other phrase, "scriptural warrant," was used in the former United Presbyterian Church in North America to indicate the need for a biblical basis for doctrine and practice. The *Book of Confessions* provides Scripture references in endnotes to the Westminster Confession suggesting that these are basic Bible references.[12]

There are two scriptural allusions given for G-4.0101. I have put in bold type the words that seem to me especially relevant to this paragraph:

Revelation 5:9 They sing a new song:
"'You are worthy to take the scroll
and to open its seals,
for you were slaughtered and by your blood
    you ransomed for God
saints **from every tribe and language and
    people and nation. . . .' "**

Acts 2:39   **"'For the promise is for you, for your
    children, and for all who are far away,
    everyone whom the Lord our God calls
    to him.'"**

G-4.0101 lays the foundation for Chapter IV. Moving to the next paragraph, we shift our theological focus.

II

G-4.0102

"Since this whole company cannot meet together in one place to worship and to serve, it is reasonable that it should be divided into particular congregations. The particular church is, therefore, understood as a local expression of the universal Church." The second paragraph, opening with the conjunction "since," signals a shift in perspective, a shift from universal to particular. We are alerted to proceed carefully into the sharp turn ahead, from theological affirmation to practical observation, from acknowledging the worldwide fellowship of Christians, to "particular congregations." The *Book of Order* makes such shifts in perspective from time to time. Ignoring such shifts produces misunderstanding and confusion.

John A. Mackay's course on "ecumenics" at Princeton Theological Seminary in the 1950s led many of us to seek to serve as pastors in the ecumenical church. We soon learned that there were no ecumenical congregations where one could be ordained.[13] Our only option was to carry the ecumenical vision into whatever denomination organized the particular churches where we could nurture our concern. It was a discovery for us that churches are particular institutions.

The introductory phrase in G-4.0102 indicates that professing Christians share a basic necessity to "meet together." By definition, a church is a faith community gathered together for specific purposes. Jesus Christ called the "Church" into being and " . . . [gives] it all that is necessary for its mission to the world, for its building up, and for its service to God"(G-1.0100b).[14]

It is evident from the New Testament that particular churches were formed as Paul and the other apostles preached the good news across the Middle East. Some epistles went to cities: Colossae, Corinth, Ephesus, Philippi, Rome, and Thessalonica. The book of Galatians was originally a letter addressed to a province of Asia Minor. John of Revelation writes special messages to seven particular churches in western Asia Minor: Ephesus, Smyrna, Pergamum, Thyatira, Sardis, Philadelphia, and Laodicea,[15] These "particular churches" came together not as institutions but as instruments to get on with the business of worship and service.

One specific instance of dealing with emerging community needs is recorded in Acts 6:1–6. Some Greek believers complained that widows were being treated unfairly in the food distribution program because of what today we call ethnic discrimination. A service function was not working properly. The twelve called a meeting and chose seven men to manage the food distribution. We have an up close and personal case of a particular community handling its affairs and dealing with controversy.

The conclusion is that particular churches are necessary. It makes sense to have these churches. This is a reasonable way to proceed. Otherwise, no way exists for believers to worship and serve together. A discussion of "reasonable" is in Chapter One of this book. Here the word means to make sense. While the Bible warrants local churches, it is also sensible that these churches exist as specific places where the faithful may gather for worship, fellowship, and mutual support.

Particularity, however, does not imply that each church is separated from the universal church. Particular churches are a part of a much larger whole. That is why we Presbyterians insist that particular churches are "understood as a local expression of the universal church." Local expression means that particular churches are free to exercise their individuality within the parameters of the wider wisdom of the universal church. This statement includes an understanding of connection that respects a range of differences of expression.

Such differences are evident in the way denominations understand how their particular local churches are connected to one another. In the Episcopal form of government, there is a "top-down" tendency in which bishops are the final determiners of doctrine and practice. The Congregational form sees each local church as the final determiner of its doctrine and practice, with local and regional associations for discussion of common issues, which lack force and effect until the local body votes to affirm a stand on those issues. Presbyterians follow the model of representative democracy, where duly elected persons meet in governing bodies to determine policy and doctrine under the terms of a constitution that spells out the spheres of authority for each level of the church. We will look at these characteristics of government later.

As persons change their membership from one denomination to another, they sometimes realize that there are different decision makers and decision-making processes. Not highlighting such differences during their transfer process may lead to confusion and distress.

"Therefore" conveys both privilege and responsibility. On the one hand, it is an honor to consider that each local church, wherever it is, whatever its size, problems, and challenges, expresses a way that the universal, eternal church speaks to and serves the people of our planet. On the other hand, there remains the call to responsibility to express the gospel in ways that conform to the witness of the church as the body of Christ in the world.

This seemingly self-evident and minor point will prove before the end of the chapter to be critically important for the life of the Presbyterian Church (U.S.A.). We are ready to shift our focus again, more narrowly this time, clarifying what "particular churches" are.

G-4.0103 Particular Church

A particular church consists of	1
those persons in a particular place,	2
along with their children,	3
who profess faith in Jesus Christ as Lord and Savior and	4
who have been gathered for the service of God	5
as set forth in Scripture,	6
subject to a particular form of church government.	7

G-4.0103 defines "particular church." If this paragraph sounds familiar, it is because lines 2–4 are very close to the wording in G-4.0101. The changes begin with the introduction in line 5 of the verb "have been gathered." Notice that the verb suggests that the persons are brought together by the Lord of the church, rather than purely by their decision. The point is that faith and profession begin with God's gracious call, not with human choice. Becoming a church member can seem paradoxical as what seems to be a personal or family decision coincides with God's call. People don't just simply begin going to church. Becoming a church member involves more than people often realize.

Many approaches to evangelism are practiced, most of them rooted in research on why people choose to attend a particular church. Some reasons are the preaching, the education, the music, the outreach, or the fellowship programs of that church. Other reasons are the architecture, the proximity to one's home, the denomination, or even a conversation with a friend or neighbor. Numerous books offer clues on how to maximize the appeal of a particular church. Sometimes evangelism seems more like marketing than anything else. While these are factors, these work only when God's grace is understood as the ultimate motivator.

The passive voice of the verb reminds us of the other dimension in the decision to affiliate with a particular church. The profession of faith is more than a formality. Public acknowledgment first before a session and then the congregation of a particular church is critical for the spiritual health of God's people.

Line 5 clarifies the purpose of the gathering: "for the service of God." This phrase reminds us of Romans 12:1: "I appeal to you therefore, brothers and sisters, by the mercies of God, to present your bodies as a living sacrifice, holy and acceptable to God, which is your spiritual worship." As explained in a footnote to this verse in the New Revised Standard Version, *spiritual* can also be translated *reasonable*, which is the adjective used in the King James Version. Eugene Peterson's translation offers a contemporary plea: "So here's what I want you to do, God helping you: Take your everyday, ordinary life—your sleeping, eating, going-to-work, and walking-around life—and place it before God as an offering."[16]

Most of us have little or no direct knowledge of servants, in the sense of the "house staff" who cared for the wealthy in earlier times. Kazuo Ishiguro's novel, *The Remains of the Day*, has shaped my own understanding. Stevens, a servant in the late 1930s in England, was proud of his skill in serving. He was also keenly aware of his place and reluctant to accept expressions of appreciation and kindness. He worked hard and had little time to himself, but he reveled in his sense of fulfilling his calling.[17]

More contemporary examples of serving are the relationships we have—brief as they usually are—with waiters in restaurants. Some are better than others. I have learned to watch how waiters go about their serving, whether they work as soloists or as members of the "wait staff." I vividly recall how pleased I once was when a waiter other than the one assigned to our table quietly refilled my water glass and then went on with other responsibilities.

A biblical portrait of a servant emerges in four passages in Isaiah (43:1–4, 49:1–6, 50:4–9, and 52:13—53:12). Since 1893 these have generally been called "The Servant Songs."[18] Biblical scholar John McKenzie interprets these passages: "The Servant poems are not predictions of the future in the simple sense. They are rather insights into the future, into the ways of God with [humankind], a projection of how judgment and salvation must be realized if they are to be realized at all."[19] McKenzie suggests that these passages refer to how God's people are to relate to those around them.

Another illustration of service is found in John 13:1–30, where Jesus washes his disciples' feet just prior to his betrayal. The disciples find this action difficult to comprehend. Jesus finishes this act of servanthood and then invites his disciples to "wash one another's feet" (John 13:14). The parable of the coming of the Kingdom in Matthew 25:1–13 expresses a similar understanding of what service to God involves.

In G-4.0103, line 7 introduces another qualification of a church, namely that it is "subject to a particular form of church government." Is this particularization really necessary? I've never really understood what people mean when they tell me, "I'm more Christian than Presbyterian." This line recognizes that there are different forms of church government, which were summarized earlier: episcopal, congregational, and presbyterian. The episcopal form draws its name from the Greek word for bishop, and claims a long history. This form is sometimes called monarchical. Bishops have authority over churches in their area. This family of churches includes Roman Catholic, Orthodox, Episcopal, and Methodist denominations. These denominations differ in their understanding of how much authority bishops have.

The second family is congregational, in which each congregation determines its own practices. This form is close to pure democracy: "one person, one vote" on all questions. Denominations in this family are United Church of Christ, Baptist, and other churches that consider themselves "independent." Churches may agree to belong to an association, as long as each church decides how to implement decisions from these advisory bodies.

The presbyterian system lies between the two other forms of church organization, embodying what is called representative democracy. This means that people elect leaders who serve in governing bodies, which are related to one another by written agreement or covenant. This is how local, state, and federal governing bodies in the United States are organized.[20]

Each of these forms of organization can claim deep biblical and historical roots. For example, the distinction between episcopal and presbyterian organization has been traced to different interpretations of Titus 1:5–9, where one finds the Greek terms *episkopos* and *presbyter* in the same verse. Each form of governmental organization is rooted in a particular understanding of covenant.

The Scripture cited in the *Book of Order* for this provision is Hebrews 8:5: "They offer worship in a sanctuary that is a sketch and shadow of the heavenly one; for Moses, when he was about to erect the tent, was warned, 'See that you make everything according to the pattern that was shown you on the mountain.'" The phrase "sketch and shadow" reminds us that denominational organizational differences are provisional.

At one time, there was a group who considered themselves "divine right Presbyterians." That such a position developed is curious in light of the passage from Hebrews, as well as G-4.0103. In addition, G-1.0302 reads: every Christian Church, or union or association of particular churches, is entitled to declare the terms of admission into its communion, and the qualifications of its ministers and members, as well as the whole system of its internal government which Christ hath appointed. . . ."

The nature of church organization is provisional—no one expression is final or ultimate. We tend to become accustomed to a "way of doing things" in the church and to resist change. The only perfect church organization will come when the vision of Revelation 21 becomes reality. Any member who has relocated to another region of the country and sought out a Presbyterian church has found that our structure does not confer uniformity of practice. An interesting dynamic occurs in the practice of church polity between what is familiar ("how we do it around here") and the discovery that being Presbyterian is wonderfully diverse, with mainstays, columns, and supporting beams all providing support in their own ways for the basic sense of family.

G-4.0104

The four sentences in this paragraph move the discussion from "particular churches" to "particular Presbyterian churches," from a general description of churches to the specific characteristics of churches related to the Presbyterian Church (U.S.A.). It is a change of focus, moving from describing the forest to considering a specific tree in the forest.

These four sentences answer four questions worth asking, questions every prospective member should be told about. The questions are:

- What holds the denomination together?
- Which officers are responsible for the government of a particular church?
- Where does the buck stop?
- What is the purpose of the particular Presbyterian church?

We hope that every Presbyterian, officer or member, would know the answers!

The first sentence of G-4.0104 states, **"Each particular church of the Presbyterian Church (U.S.A.) shall be governed by this Constitution."** The Preface to the *Book of Order* notes that shall is an imperative word for Presbyterians. It signifies "practice that is mandated." We find the definition of "this Constitution" in G-1.0500: *"The Constitution of the Presbyterian Church (U.S.A.) consists of The Book of Confessions and the Book of Order."* As the United States of America is governed by a constitution, so is the Presbyterian Church (U.S.A.). There are certainly many differences in content, style, and language, but both rely on documents that set forth a structure and specific provisions to which those who govern are held to account. The two documents of the *Constitution of the Presbyterian Church (U.S.A.)* offer statements of how Presbyterians approach the Christian faith (theology) and how Presbyterians organize ourselves (polity). Since we are both a social and a theological group, Presbyterians have one document about what we believe and another about how our form of organization derives from our convictions. G-2.0100b indicates that the purpose of *The Book of Confessions* is to "identify the church as a community of people known by its convictions as well as by its actions."

Some question why Presbyterians would call this a constitution, since our documents are so much longer than the "Constitution of the United States of America." Not all constitutions are similar in language and content. One definition of constitution is "a written instrument embodying the rules of a political or social organization" (definition 5b).[21]

Where is the Bible in all this? In the *Book of Order* there are numerous references to Scripture. The terms "Word" or "the Word" are found n G-1.0100b and c, G-1.0301a, "Holy Scriptures" appear in G-1.0306 and .0307, G-2.0100b, .0200, .0300, .0400. G-3.0100 offers a succinct summary of the witness of the Bible.

The following sentence identifies those persons responsible for complying with the Constitution. The officers of a particular church **"are ministers of the Word and Sacrament, elders, and deacons."** The job descriptions for these three types of officers is the subject of Chapter VI of the *Book of Order*. The intervening chapter discusses the role of members.

Eight of the nine ordination vows these officers take are the same. These questions are the basis for the responsibility each person accepts as an officer. It is only the ninth question, identifying the office to which the person is ordained, that is different. Beyond the session of the local church, officers bear equal authority in governing. Their votes are of equal weight. Officers are chosen by the members of the church, a principle that was articulated in 1789 at the first General Assembly (G-1.0306).

The first question posed at the beginning of this section was, "What holds the Presbyterian Church together?" While various answers have been given over the years, I propose that it is the faithfulness of those who have taken ordination vows. Since there are many more elders than ministers of the Word and Sacrament, it is correct to say, "faithful Presbyterian elders." Not only are there more elders than ministers, elders tend to remain in particular churches longer than pastors. A session consists of the elders currently serving, plus a moderator, who is usually the pastor (G-10.0100).

Presbytery also plays an important role in holding the Presbyterian Church together. Presbytery is the next governing body above the session, where ministers have their membership and the work of sessions is initially reviewed. Presbytery is where ministers and commissioned elders from each church share in the governance of those churches within the bounds of that presbytery.

Moving to the second question at the beginning of this section, the officers of the church are ministers of the Word and Sacrament and elders and deacons. Their ordination vows make it clear that they are responsible for the "peace, unity, and purity" of the church, a Presbyterian way of speaking about their duty.

This leads us to the third question, "Where does the buck stop?" The short answer is, "By and large, with the session." The text of the relevant paragraph in the *Book of Order* is, **"Its government and guidance are the responsibility of the session"** (G-4.0104). The session makes decisions about how a church goes about its life and mission. The congregation votes on five issues, including who the officers of the church will be. Otherwise, the session is the governing body, responsible for all decisions regarding what the church does and does not do, within the guidelines of the *Constitution*. One indication of the session's authority is the assigned nineteen responsibilities given it for the local church (G-10.0102). The presupposition for this arrangement is set forth in G-7.0103: "The law and government of the Presbyterian Church (U.S.A.) presuppose the fellowship of women and men with their children in voluntary covenanted relationship with one another and with God through Jesus Christ. The organization rests upon the fellowship and is not designed to work without trust and love."

Another facet of the Presbyterian process of local church government is review. Review is the referral of decisions of governing bodies and individual persons to other governing bodies, with final resolution resting with the governing body doing the review. Two review processes, administrative and disciplinary, are possible. "Administrative review" is similar to an annual medical check-up. The review provides an opportunity for the session and the presbytery to see that affairs are being properly conducted. A major part of this is the review of the minutes of the session by the presbytery (G-9.0407). "Special administrative review" (G-9.0408—.0411), which could be likened to an annual physical that leads to a trip to the hospital, is available.

The other form of review is the formal disciplinary process, which follows "The Rules of Discipline." The first chapter (D-1.0000) is the preamble for this section of the *Book of Order*. Because it deals with rules to be followed, the language is precise and the words technical.

Finally, we arrive at the question, "Why particular Presbyterian churches?" The response is simply, that each church **"shall fulfill its responsibilities as the local unit of mission for the service of all people, for the upbuilding of the whole church, and for the glory of God"** (G-4.0104). A particular Presbyterian church is the basic unit of mission. A thoughtful reading of G-3.0000 offers a comprehensive presentation of what a church is called to be and do.[22]

This chapter opened with reflection on the first section of G-4.0000 and the consideration of the church of Jesus Christ around the world and throughout the ages, what the historic creeds call "the communion of saints." We moved to the need for particular churches, where these saints gather to worship and serve the Lord of the church. Finally, we have arrived at the relationship of specific churches to the Presbyterian Church (U.S.A.) and have focused on how we Presbyterians have chosen to serve as a specific community within the broader framework with which we began.

This has been a "distinctively Presbyterian" movement. An early form of cooperation was the "Plan of Union" between the General Association of Connecticut and the General Assembly approved in 1802 " 'to prevent alienation, and to promote union and harmony in those new settlements which are composed of inhabitants from these bodies.' " The Plan continued in operation until 1837.[23] Who was the General Association of Connecticut? Was this a Presbyterian body?

In July 1875 a delegation of twelve persons appointed by the 1875 General Assembly went to London and assisted in forming the Alliance of Presbyterian and Reformed Churches. Included in the constitution adopted at that meeting is this agreement of twenty-two Presbyterian organizations:

> In forming this Alliance the Presbyterian Churches do not mean to change their fraternal relations with other Churches, but will be ready, as heretofore, to join with them in Christian fellowship, and in advancing the cause of the Redeemer, on the general principle maintained and taught in the Reformed Confessions, that the Church of God on earth, though composed of many members, is one body in the communion of the Holy Ghost, of which body Christ is the supreme Head, and the Scriptures alone are the infallible law.[24]

Subsequently, Presbyterians have participated in the formation of ecumenical enterprises, such as the National Council of Churches of Christ in the U.S.A. and the World Council of Churches.

Notes

1. The *Shorter Oxford English Dictionary on Historical Principles*, vol. 2, 5th edition (Oxford, UK: Oxford University Press, 2002), p. 2358.
2. The Westminster Confession of Faith, *The Constitution of the Presbyterian Church (U.S.A.). Part 1: The Book of Confessions.* (Louisville: Office of the General Assembly, 1999), 6.141.
3. *Book of Confessions, Study Edition*, p. 204.
4. The concept in this paragraph is a unique theological understanding. The Westminster Confession of Faith, 6.140.
5. The Westminster Confession of Faith, 6.146–148.
6. "Catholic" not capitalized refers to all expressions of Christianity worldwide. The Roman Catholic Church is understood as one of these expressions. The word "catholic" comes from two Greek words, meaning "of the whole world."
7. The Westminster Confession of Faith, 6.144.
8. The Scots Confession, 3.18.
9. Ibid.
10. *Book of Order 2004/2005, Part II*, footnote at the end of the "Scriptural Allusion Index."
11. Jack B. Rogers and Donald K. McKim, *The Authority and Interpretation of the Bible: An Historical Approach* (San Francisco: Harper & Row, 1979), p. 201. The authors add that, "The Divines were reluctant, fearing misuse of the method of citing proof texts."
12. A General Note in the *Book of Confessions: Study Edition* introduces these references: "At several points the Confession of Faith is more specific in its statements than the Scriptures. These statements are inferences drawn from the Scriptures or from statements based on the Scriptures, or from the experience and observation of the Church. In such cases no texts are cited, but reference is made to this General Note" (p. 217).
13. A few ecumenical churches under the aegis of the National Council of Churches are in foreign countries and are often called "American churches."
14. Chapter III in the *Book of Order* is titled, "The Church and Its Mission." For a further discussion of this material, see William E. Chapman, *Mission Symphony: Notes for the Third Millennium* (Louisville: Witherspoon Press, 2004).
15. Revelation, chapters 2—3. The "Scriptural Allusions" for G-4.0102 refer to Galatians 1:21, 22 and Revelations 2:1. The text goes beyond this skeletal reference.
16. Eugene Peterson, *The Message: The New Testament in Contemporary Language* (Colorado Springs: Navpress, 1993), p. 328.
17. Kazuo Ishgura, *The Remains of the Day* (New York: Vintage Books, A Division of Random House, Inc.), 1989.

18. John L. McKenzie, *The Anchor Bible: Second Isaiah* (Garden City, NY: Doubleday & Company, Inc., 1968), p. xxxviii.
19. Ibid., p. iv.
20. The connection between covenant theology and the American system of government is explored in a way I find instructive and persuasive in Charles S. McCoy and J. Wayne Baker, *Fountainhead of Federalism: Heinrich Bullinger and the Covenantal Tradition* (Louisville: Westminster/John Knox Press, 1991).
21. *Webster's New Collegiate Dictionary* (Springfield, MA: G. &. C. Merriam Co., 1980), p. 241.
22. For a study of this chapter, see my *Mission Symphony: Notes for the Third Millennium* (Louisville: Witherspoon Press), 2004.
23. J. Aspinwall Hodge, *What Is Presbyterian Law as Defined by The Church Courts?*, 8th edition (Philadelphia: Presbyterian Board of Publication and Sabbath-School Work, 1907), pp. 277–279.
24. *The Historical Sections of the Digest: United Presbyterian Church of North America and Presbyterian Church in the United States of America to May 27, 1958* (Philadelphia: The Office of the General Assembly by the Board of Christian Education, The United Presbyterian Church in the U.S.A.).

TWO

The Unity
of the Church

━━⟨⟨⟨⟩⟩⟩━━

That a discussion of "the unity of the Church" follows imme-
diately after an exploration of "the particular church" illustrates the Presbyterian tendency toward complexity. The
theological concept of unity balances the practical tone of chapter II. At the same time, the tension between the universal and
the particular church continues in the background.

Many consider unity a controversial aspect of current Presbyterian life. It is ironic that unity has been such a contentious
topic. This second step in exploring Presbyterian life raises the
question: "What sort of unity?" The answer provides us with
three aspects of unity, each carefully discussed: unity in mission;
unity as oneness; visible unity.

G-4.0201 Unity in Mission

**"The unity of the Church is a gift of its Lord and finds
expression in its faithfulness to the mission to which Christ
calls it. The Church is a fellowship of believers which seeks
the enlargement of the circle of faith to include all people and
is never content to enjoy the benefits of Christian community
for itself alone."**

Unity in the Presbyterian lexicon has two characteristics,
according to the first sentence of G-4.0201. It is God's gift to
the church universal. As with all gifts, it is up to the recipient
to determine whether and how to use what has been given.
Gift becomes responsibility. The recipient is challenged to use
whatever is given in such a way that the giver is respected
and honored.

Early in the *Book of Order*, we learn that, "Christ calls the Church into being, giving it all that is necessary" (G-1.0100b). One of the prayers of confession in the 1946 *Book of Common Worship* admits the sin of wasting God's gifts and forgetting God's love.[1] The rejection of God's gift of unity is one that we seldom acknowledge when we confess our sins. Yet exclusion of others is a corporate sin for which each of us is more or less responsible.

This leads us to ask, "How should we use this gift of unity?" The answer appears in the next clause, where the gift, finds expression in its faithfulness to the mission to which Christ calls it. "Finds expression" is an easily remembered term that is critical for faithfulness. How do we as Christians personally and corporately express our faith and our gratitude to God, using those distinctive talents that are ours because God has given them to us and has enabled us to develop them so that we may more winsomely testify to God's amazing grace in Jesus Christ?

Mission is one of those words that is so huge in its implications that we are tempted again and again to cut it down to size, to something that engages our particular understanding. Defining mission has been a continuing battleground of particular churches, presbyteries, synods, as well as our denomination. The temptation is to take our own or our groups' understanding and advocate that a particular piece of mission should be what everyone should be doing. Consequently, we find ourselves squabbling about which mission should get how much emphasis and funding, while the mission to which we are called goes undone. Lord, have mercy upon us!

The next sentence indicates the mission to which the church is called. The church is called "a fellowship of believers." This characterization picks up on the earlier statement in G-4.0101 that the church consists of persons who "commit themselves to live in fellowship under [Christ's] rule." While we have standards for life in the church, we also have the dynamic of fellowship that engages the whole person. Presbyterians have a reputation for being standoffish, which gets in the way of becoming a fellowship. Our *Book of Order* reminds us that our churches need to be fellowships if we are to be faithful.

This fellowship has been given an assignment, in both a positive and a negative sense. On the positive side, the fellowship "seeks the enlargement of the circle of faith to include all people."

This phrase deftly brings together traditional evangelism and the social witness aspect of mission. Conversion for many carries overtones of manipulation or coercion. Such overtones or understandings result from what may have been excessive zeal, if not displaced aggression, in many missionary efforts in the past. The beauty of the phrase, "seeks the enlargement of the circle of faith" is its softness, which arises from the humble desire to share a distinctive quality of life.

To "include all people" (G-4.0200) in the circle of faith extends to all humanity the experience of being touched by grace. Presbyterians are still predominantly Anglo-Saxon in spite of attempts to reach out to all ethnicities of newcomers to our country. We need to recognize and lament our past ineptitude in this area, reaching out to those whose backgrounds differ from our own, even as we continue to work out ways in which we can be more faithful ourselves.

We have done better in reaching out to other countries. Increasingly, we are discovering how our foreign mission enterprise of years past is now delivering to our doorsteps brothers and sisters from other cultures with other traditions—people who are eager to share their gifts with us, to God's greater glory.

A paradox is inherent in mission, which has continued to trouble Presbyterians since early times. Both the Old Side–New Side division of 1745–1758 and the Old School–New School division of 1837–1870 resulted from disputes about the proper balance between personal evangelism and social witness. Those who contend that this controversy is recent are apparently unfamiliar with our history.[2] We have apparently been slow learners. We resemble the church in Corinth to which Paul wrote: "Now I appeal to you, brothers and sisters, by the name of our Lord Jesus Christ, that all of you should be in agreement and that there should be no divisions among you, but that you should be united in the same mind and the same purpose" (1 Cor. 1:10). Presbyterian controversies persist at every level of life in the church—interpersonal, local church, presbytery, synod, General Assembly. When will we be ready to live out our mission in the sense that each of us offers our gifts to God's greater glory through the mercy and grace of Jesus Christ?

The paragraph in G-.4.0201 concludes: "and is never content to enjoy the benefits of Christian community for itself alone."

Expanding the circle of faith requires us to go beyond our personal comfort zone, to listen to one another carefully and respectfully, understanding that God's Spirit often addresses us through the lips of our brother or sister. Our motto of "'The church reformed, always reforming', according to the Word of God and the call of the Spirit" (G-2.0200) is lived out as we engage in the pilgrimage of faith through openness to others. The state of being discontented might be paraphrased as a holy restlessness. The challenge is to discern whether the restlessness is holy or otherwise. We find a guide in the "Historic Principles of Church Order" quoting the Bible, "'By their fruits ye shall know them'" (G-1.0304).

The covenant that binds Presbyterians together rests on the new covenant that Jesus Christ has given us, essentially, "that you love one another, as I have loved you" (John 15:12). Mission is energized when the circle expands through sharing Christ's love for each of us. Love such as this is best exhibited when the circle of faith expands. Numbers are not the only (and perhaps potentially misleading) measures of effectiveness.

G-4.0202

"There is one Church. As the Bible speaks of the one body which is the Church living under the one Spirit of God known through Christ, it reminds us that we have "'one Lord, one faith, one baptism, one God and Father of us all.' (Ephesians 4:5–6)."

The four-word sentence that opens G-4.0202 distills what has led up to it. Its simplicity and directness add weight to this affirmation. The progression has led from the universal to the particular church, including consideration of how churches differ yet are similar within a larger unity. Different ways of organizing church life are evident. We choose one of the options open to us, without losing sight that we are one church.

The vocabulary changes from "unity" to "oneness" between the first and second paragraphs. Is this simply a change of wording, or is it a subtle signal? I suggest that the shift is from ordinary church language to the scriptural word. We confess in the Apostles' Creed that we believe "in one holy catholic Church." The Nicene Creed adds two words, "in one holy catholic and apostolic church. . . ." This is the way the Apostle Paul refers to the church, as this paragraph reminds us.

Now we come to the heart of the matter: "There is *one* Church" (author's emphasis). This expression strikes me almost as a challenge. I hear an overtone of, "What part of 'one Church' don't you understand?" I am caught up short by such a simple declaration, after following the complexities of concepts in multi-phrase sentences. This sentence comes as a sudden burst of radiance, one that startles even as I am confronted with its power.

This affirmation leads me to ask, "How can this be, with all the various churches contending that each one is more faithful to the gospel than the others?" As if expecting such astonishment, the text continues with the reassuring phrase, "As the Bible speaks of one body . . . ." The affirmation of unity which follows comes from Ephesians 4:5–6: "one Lord, one faith, one baptism, one God and Father of all. . . ." This reference is offered as a reminder, suggesting that we sometimes fail to remember Paul's affirmation.

Leading into the reference, we find that a critical assumption is identified, namely: "living under the one Spirit of God known through Christ" (G-4.0202). What amazes me is the focus of this phrase, on how we live. While there is some concern for doctrinal correctness, a hallmark of Presbyterian rectitude, there is also stress on how what we believe informs how we go about the business of living out our faith, presenting another Presbyterian paradox.

An elder of Messiah Presbyterian Church in Lubbock, Texas, introduced me to the way African American Presbyterians put it: "It's one thing to talk the talk and something else to walk the walk." This echoes the prophet Micah who preached that God's people are called "to do justice, and to love kindness, and to walk humbly with your God?" (Mic. 6:8). We are all pilgrims, humbly following our Risen Lord.

G-4.0203 Visible Oneness

Visible oneness, by which a diversity of persons, gifts, and understandings is brought together, is an important sign of the unity of God's people. It is also a means by which that unity is achieved. Further, while divisions into different denominations do not destroy this unity, they do obscure it for both the Church and the world. The Presbyterian Church (U.S.A.), affirming its historical continuity with the whole Church of Jesus Christ, is committed to the reduction of that obscurity and is willing to seek and to maintain communion and community with all other branches of the one, catholic Church (G-15.0000).

The final section of G-4.0200 moves toward a resolution of a tension that has shadowed discussion of the chapter up to now. The shift is from biblical and theological unity to an observable reality: "visible oneness." The definition of oneness, which to this point has been missing, comes as a dependent phrase: "by which a diversity of persons, gifts, and understandings is brought together. . . ."

This phrase adds another level of meaning to the assertion in G-4.0201, "The unity of the Church is a gift. . . ." God's grace provides that "a diversity of persons, gifts, and understandings is brought together . . . (G-4.0203)." Visible oneness is presented as discernible evidence of God's blessing. God's grace infuses human witness, in such a way that understanding the basis for such unity is essential for those who find themselves working toward increasing the degree of "being together."

Our *Book of Order* discusses fellowship as visible oneness in the unique sense of the word that is appropriate for the church. Fellowship is such a useful word that it is now used in common speech, with the result that its meaning has become blurred. The New Testament Greek word for fellowship is κοινονια (koinonia). Both fellowship and *koinonia* are used in the church with various meanings, resulting in confusion.

Attempting to provide some insight into the depth of the meaning of *koinonia*, New Testament scholar Gerhard Lohfink in his book *Jesus and Community* suggests a linguistic clue to the unique quality of relationships in the church by pointing to an overlooked pronoun that appears in the New Testament 87 times.[3] This pronoun, αλλελον, is reciprocal, denoting mutual connection and care.

Lohfink also finds another key term in the word "edification." He suggests that Paul understood his role in building up the church as fulfilling Jeremiah's wording of God's promise to the people of Judah that they would return to their land (Jer. 24:5–7). He goes on to quote Philip Vielhauer: "The goal of the ways of God is not the pious individual, but the one, holy, catholic church, in the pregnant and radically eschatological sense of the New Testament; it is the church's creation and preservation, its promotion and realization, that Paul describes as *oikodomein*" [edification].[4]

Vielhauer raises the issue of the scope of edification and by so doing corrects a solely individualistic understanding of edification.

Paul's prayer in his letter to the church in Rome addresses this issue similarly: "May the God of steadfastness and encouragement grant you to live in harmony with one another, in accordance with Christ Jesus, so that together you may with one voice glorify the God and Father of our Lord Jesus Christ" (Rom. 15:5–6).

My wife and I are related to a church whose sanctuary was destroyed by fire in January 2003. The West Side Presbyterian Church in Ridgewood, New Jersey is rebuilding the worship space from the ground up, a process that involves much energy, and time, not to mention money. About a hundred people are directly involved in the work of physical rebuilding. What is interesting is that there is also a committee assigned to the spiritual rebuilding, asking such questions as: What will the congregation do with the new structure? What new ministries is this congregation called to? How can the "new" church be ready for a new sense of mission and ministry?

Both Scripture and the *Book of Order* remind us that "building up the Body of Christ" is always in order, yet too frequently left aside as we do what we consider church work. In relation to this enterprise, we would do well to keep in mind one final warning from Psalm 127: "Unless the LORD builds the house, those who build it labor in vain."

Diversity is a reminder that "building the Body" is more than adding bodies. While membership numbers remind us of one way in which we are being challenged, perhaps the Lord of the church is reminding us that there is an even more pressing responsibility, one that might be called spiritual maintenance. More numbers may or may not indicate the degree of faithfulness of a particular church in fulfilling the mission to which it is called.

For now the focus is on the breadth of the meaning of being called to the unity of the body of Christ. This is especially important in our age in which consumerism seems to have more devotees than churches. The issue is God's call "to a new openness to its own membership, by affirming itself as a community of diversity . . . ." (G-3.0401b). The challenge is to understand this provision as applying to particular congregations, presbyteries, synods, and the General Assembly, as well as beyond the borders of our denomination.

The next sentence of G-4.0203 is: **"It [visible oneness] is also a means by which that unity is achieved."** At first glance, this sentence is hardly worth a second glance, almost a throw-away line. How does it contribute to the discussion?

The fulcrum for the sentence is **"a means."** A fulcrum works two ways. Visible oneness is not an end in itself but a means to accomplish something else. Putting too much stress on visible oneness risks turning what is intended to be a contributing quality into an end or criterion by which a church is evaluated. To turn a means into an end is to endanger the larger goal.

On the other hand, aspiring to **"visible oneness"** *is* one way to move toward fulfilling Jesus' prayer, "that they may be one . . . ." (John 17:11). The social dimension of humanity is intimated in Genesis 2:18, where God says according to a recent translation, "It is not good for the human to be alone. I shall make him a sustainer beside him."[5]

It is difficult to talk about visible oneness when behavior tells another story. The next sentence points out another two-edged implication of Presbyterian understanding of visible oneness: **"Further, while divisions into different denominations do not destroy this unity, they do obscure it for both the Church and the world"** (G-4.0203). Denominations are a fact of life for American Protestant Christians—and unavoidable. The roots of denominations lie deep in our history: including an openness to, if not a welcoming of, people from numerous national and racial backgrounds; our paradoxical commitment to national unity as well as to individual freedom; and our tendency to move on as a means to resolve differences.

The facticity of Protestant denominations, as well as other branches of Christian churches, lurks behind any discussion of the unity of the church. The *Book of Order* brings this shadow into the light by acknowledging denominational diversity of belief and practice. What are we to make of this discordant reality?

The response has two points. On the one hand, the reality of denominations **"do(es) not destroy this unity."** This is not an opinion that arose in the twentieth century with the emergence of the ecumenical movement. Rather, this position reflects both Scots Confession of 1560.[6] The emphasis is on unity as a theological rather than as an empirical concept. Although it is not yet a reality that we experience, the unity is real in Christ and is an end or aim toward which we strive.

On the other hand, denominations **"obscure it [this unity], for both the Church and the world"** (G-4.0203). To a world convinced that "seeing is believing," the proliferation of denominations clouds awareness of the unity of the church. A further complication arises when some believers vigorously affirm that their church is the true church. Disunity in any guise limits witness. When churches quarrel, the double effect is to impede our witness to the gospel of Jesus Christ to the world and to divert the energy of Christians from demonstrating provisionally what God intends for all humanity (G-3.0200). When a group mobilizes people and resources to contest for or protest against some aspect of mission in the name of faith, a sad irony is on display.

The final sentence of G-4.0203, concluding the discussion of "visible oneness," sums up in one sentence our denominational position on unity. The subject of the sentence is **"The Presbyterian Church (U.S.A.),"** the official corporate name of our denomination. Two major clauses follow, setting out where we stand as a church.

The first phrase is hardly a surprise, in light of what we have seen up to now in this chapter: **"affirming its historical continuity with the whole Church of Jesus Christ . . . "** (G-4.0203). The discussion of unity has presented the scriptural and confessional basis for understanding that the church of Jesus Christ is one church. Now we as a denomination assert in our *Book of Order* that we continue in the faith of Jesus Christ.

Our history as a denomination has generally been one of cooperation with other groups of Christians. In specific instances we have gone our own way, especially during the colonial period, when the colonies were struggling with identity issues of many sorts. Beginning in 1804, with our Plan of Union with the Congregational Church regarding settling churches on the frontier, we have sought to work with others for the sake of the gospel.

Since then cooperation with other denominations has continued, sometimes with stress and disappointment. Continually we have sought to acknowledge the benefits of understanding that our oneness exceeds our particularity. For example, Southern Presbyterians resisted joining the World Alliance of Reformed Churches, which was formed in 1876. Moses Drury Hoge, pastor of Second Presbyterian Church in Richmond, Virginia, said on the floor of the Presbyterian Church of the United States General Assembly during the debate: "If we alone constitute the true church; if this only is the result of the stupendous sacrifice on Calvary and the struggles of apostles, and missionaries and reformers in all generations; then may God have mercy on the world and on his church."[7] His speech convinced the General Assembly to join the Alliance.

The next clause in this sentence affirms that the Presbyterian Church (U.S.A.) **"is committed to the reduction of that obscurity. . ."** (G-4.0203). This commitment has deep roots. For example, Theodore Beza, successor to John Calvin in Geneva and France, prepared a *Harmony of Confessions* in 1581 as a demonstration that fifteen Protestant catechisms and confessional statements expressed "the theological unity they had in Christ."[8]

The previous points from our American experience support this affirmation as consistent with our heritage. When one goes to the denominational web site www.pcusa.org, there is a link on the first page, "Who We Are." At the bottom is the category, "Ecumenical Relationships and Organizations." Click on "Ecumenical Relationships" for information about our denomination's partnership ministries abroad.

Worldwide Ministries Division (WMD) of the PC(USA) organizes relationships with partner churches and organizations in approximately 80 countries and has appointed mission personnel to serve in nearly 70 countries. WMD's area offices build and maintain relationships with Presbyterian, Reformed, and other churches around the world.

Other listings indicate organizations with whom we are related by action of the General Assembly. These are, at the time of writing:

- Department of Ecumenical and Agency Relationships
- Churches Uniting in Christ
- National Council of Churches
- World Alliance of Reformed Churches
- World Council of Churches
- Church World Service
- Ecunet
- Bossey Ecumenical Institute
- Taize

The Presbyterian Church is deeply committed to highlighting the unity of Christians. Personal ecumenical commitments go well beyond these few.

The *Book of Order* contains further evidence of this commitment. Chapter XV of the Form of Government, titled "Relationships," begins with a five-paragraph section called "Ecumenical Commitment." The second section (G-15.0200) discusses "Relations with Other Denominations." The chapter concludes with provisions for "Church Union." Chapter XVI relates to "Union Churches" while Chapter XVII deals with "Union Governing Bodies."

Three of the six appendices contain ecumenical documents further showing the commitment to ecumenism. Appendix B is the "Articles of Agreement" reuniting the United Presbyterian Church in the United States of America with the Presbyterian Church in the United States in 1983, healing a division since 1861. Article 12 of these Articles deals with "Ecumenical Relationships" in order to ensure continuity of these ties.

In Appendix C we find "A Formula of Agreement between the Evangelical Lutheran Church in America, the Presbyterian Church (U.S.A.), the Reformed Church in America, and the United Church of Christ on Entering into Full Communion on the Basis of *A Common Calling*." This document was approved by the 209th General Assembly (1997) and declared part of the *Book of Order* by the 210th General Assembly (1998). The ten pages in this document set forth how these four denominations understand their relationship with one another.

We then come to Appendix D, which contains three parts: The first is "Visible Marks of Churches Uniting in Christ," identifying nine visible marks of the relationship. "The Official Text Report of the Eighteenth Plenary of the Consultation on Church Union," which gathered in 1999 is followed by "Call to Christian Commitment and Action to Combat Racism," also adopted at the eighteenth plenary in 1999.

These documents included in the *Book of Order* for all to see support the commitment to unity in diversity. These documents also provide a basis for looking at the last clause of G-4.0203: **"and is willing to seek and to maintain communion and community with all other branches of the one, catholic Church. (G-15.0000)."**

"Seek" and "maintain" are calls to work at reconciliation between estranged groups of Christians. When elders and ministers vow in their ordination to "further the peace, unity, and purity of the church," they are committing themselves to continuing to seek fulfillment of the prayer of Jesus Christ, "that they [who believe in me through the word] may be one, as we are one" (John 17:22). Too often this vow has been taken and soon forgotten or else misinterpreted.

Princeton seminarians in the late 1950s were required to take a course in ecumenics, taught by President John A. Mackay. The course showed us how the ecumenical movement emerged from concerns of missionaries. One of the ironies of history is the way mission concerns led some to distrust ecumenical organizations in the later years of the twentieth century. Mackay himself had been a missionary in Brazil, and his experience in that country continued to inform his understanding and drive as a Presbyterian ecumenical leader. I recall him saying that his involvement in ecumenical circles made him feel at once both more and less Presbyterian. He seemed both to be embracing the commitment to work for cooperation in an attempt to make the unity of the church less obscure and contributing the particular gifts of our denomination to the ongoing process of mission.

Dr. Mackay's remark demonstrates his ability to maintain both a focus on the specific and an awareness of the importance of the context of the whole picture within which the specific is located. Some call this a systems perspective. For Presbyterians, it is one of the continuing challenges as we seek to live out our faith. As we turn to the next chapter, we will need to bear in mind what we have just learned.

Notes

1. *The Book of Common Worship* (Philadelphia: Board of Christian Education, 1946), p. 12.
2. For example, James H. Smylie, *A Brief History of the Presbyterians* (Louisville: Geneva Press, 1996).
3. Gerhard Lohfink, *Jesus and Community: The Social Dimension of Christian Faith,* trans. John P. Galvin (Philadelphia: Fortress Press, 1984). This discussion begins on p. 99.

4. Ibid., p. 102. The reference is to Vielhauer's article, "OIKODOMEE: Das Bild vom Bau in der christlichen Literatur vom Neuen Testament bis Clemens Alexandrinus." In *Oikodome: Aufsätzee Neuen Testament*, 2:1—168 (Munich: Chr. Kaiser, 1979).
5. Robert Alter, *The Five Books of Moses: A Translation with Commentary* (New York: W. W. Norton & Company, 2004), pp. 21–22.
6. The Scots Confession, *The Book of Confessions*, 3.18.
7. James H. Smylie, *A Brief History of the Presbyterians* (Louisville: Geneva Press, 1996), p. 92.
8. Ibid., p. 25.

THREE

Nine Principles of Presbyterian Government

W e have arrived at the heart of the matter: foundational assumptions for how the Presbyterian Church (U.S.A.) is meant to operate. The title of G-4.0300, "Principles of Presbyterian Government," announces a shift in focus from general context to specific provisions: **"The Presbyterian Church (U.S.A.) reaffirms, within the context of its commitment to the Church universal, a special commitment to basic principles of Presbyterian polity. . . ."**

These principles are the hallmarks of Presbyterian practice. The word "hallmark" derives from the practice of English goldsmiths of putting a distinctive mark on each piece produced by a member of the guild. This mark indicated that the guild had authorized particular smiths to create pieces and trusted that they would do quality work consistent with their personal reputation. In like manner, failure of a church session or a pastor to abide by the following principles signals a departure from Presbyterian "good practice."

Presbyterian polity is located **"within the context of its commitment to the Church universal."** Such an affirmation answers the question of why in this particular part of the *Book of Order* the apparent side trip into ecumenical matters is so evident. We have shifted gears, returning to the way particular Presbyterian churches and the governing entities of our denomination are to go about being church.

The term **"special commitment"** underscores the importance of the nine principles of our polity that follow. This phrase also points to the fact that the principles are grounded deeply in Scripture and in the creeds and confessions that are included in our *Book of Confessions*. When officers respond affirmatively to the question set forth in "Will you be governed by our church's polity, and will you abide by its discipline?" (G.-14.0207e), they are acknowledging the serious nature of this section of the *Book of Order*.

The term **"Basic principles"** further emphasizes the importance of these nine statements. We are now at ground level, exploring the practical, day-by-day footings for the work of the Presbyterian Church (U.S.A.) in each of its entities. The principles are also basic in the sense that the wording is straightforward, which tempts us to quickly scan each principle and assume that we now know it and will behave accordingly. Reflection, however, requires a slower pace, a willingness to ponder and to live with the meaning of the words, to allow it to speak to our deeper selves, and to inform how we personally go about our church work, whatever form that takes.

One may ask, "How are these principles related to the rest of the *Constitution of the Presbyterian Church (U.S.A.)*?" One answer is that these form a bridge between theological understandings and the practicalities of life in community. Some of the principles appear to be so simple that we may have a tendency to say, "That goes without saying." However, experience has taught Presbyterians that not observing these principles results in tension. Upon these principles rests the specific characterization of how Presbyterians go about being church.

The final two words of introduction for this chapter are **"Presbyterian polity."** "Polity" is derived from the Greek word for city. It differs from the more familiar word politics in the sense that polity refers to how a community's affairs are ordered, while politics refers to how things get done in a community. While it is not correct to say that polity is purely a Presbyterian word, Presbyterians are in fact the ones who use it in church life.

The first principle of Presbyterian polity is, **"The particular churches of the Presbyterian Church (U.S.A.) wherever they are, taken collectively, constitute one church . . . "** (G-4.0301a). We remember from G-4.0103 the definition of a particular, or local church: "A particular church consists of those persons in a particular place, along with their children, who profess faith in Jesus

Christ as Lord and Savior and who have been gathered for the service of God as set forth in Scripture, subject to a particular form of church government." In his 1907 book on Presbyterian polity for elders and deacons, J. Aspinwall Hodge offered another definition of particular church:

> A particular Presbyterian church, so far as adults are concerned, is constituted and organized, as such, by a number of individuals professing to walk together as the disciples of Jesus Christ, on the principles of the 'Confession of Faith' and 'Form of Government of the Presbyterian Church,' and the election and ordination of one or more Ruling Elders, who, by the ordination-service, become the spiritual rulers of the persons voluntarily submitting themselves to their authority in the Lord.[1]

The term particular church has been used by Presbyterians for more than a century, and thus it is appropriate that this distinctive phrase is used in our denomination, **Presbyterian Church (U.S.A.)**.

The next words are **"wherever they are."** When I did staff work for our denomination, I was seldom able to determine where a telephone call originated. These calls helped me appreciate the scope of diversity of the Presbyterian Church (U.S.A.). Attending meetings of the General Assembly is another way to encounter the spread of our church across the United States. "Wherever they are" also alerts us to other ways of locating particular churches. The neighborhoods where one finds Presbyterian churches differ enormously. Many of the popular Presbyterian stereotypes have little factual basis. As we discover how diverse we are as Presbyterians, some fear that we are no longer true to our heritage. Others find increasing diversity to give credence to our motto in G-2.0200, "The church reformed, [is] always reforming."

"Wherever they are" reminds us that there is no cookie cutter sense of how a church lives out its faith. Styles of worship, hymnbooks, architecture, and theological bent are some of the possible characteristics that can identify particular churches. As one travels to different parts of the country, these differences soon become evident.

This first principle ends with the words **"constitute one church."** These three words are critically important, yet seldom understood. The implications of **"constitute one church"** are multiple and far-reaching.

The General Assembly Permanent Judicial Commission (GAPJC) referenced this provision in a 1992 decision. A church session decided not to pay the per capita assessment because they felt that "the General Assembly, the Synod of the Northeast, and our own Presbytery of Long Island have adopted policies and supported causes where we no longer in good conscience can be a part of supporting."[2]   The GAPJC responded in its decision, commenting that "We proclaim and take seriously the notion of one church (G-4.0301a). While our *Book of Order* speaks in terms of "higher governing bodies" (G-4.0301f), we acknowledge that our system contemplates a partnership of church governance in which each governing body has responsibilities, exercises authority, and carries out mission in particular areas (G–9.0103).[3]

The congregation of each particular church makes decisions in five specific areas about its leaders and some aspects of its property (G-7.0304). The *Book of Order* also defines areas of responsibility for each level of the church. The *Constitution* sets forth the terms of the partnership, so that all Presbyterians can become aware of how we serve together.

While particular Presbyterian churches seeking a pastor have one pool of candidates eligible for a call, most other denominations restrict the scope of search for a pastor to those in a specific region of the country.

Another implication of **"constitute one church"** is found in G-8.0201, a one sentence paragraph seventy-eight words longs. The heart of the sentence is "All [church] property . . . is held in trust nevertheless for the use and benefit of the Presbyterian Church (U.S.A.)." The intervening words define "all" so that the provision means what it says. Other denominations have similar language, so this is not unique to the Presbyterian Church (U.S.A.).

The second principle leads us into yet another implication of "one church," which is seldom noticed yet important for how we Presbyterians go about being church. The second principle is: **"This church shall be governed by presbyters (elders and ministers of the Word and Sacrament, traditionally called ruling and teaching elders)."** (G-4.0301b)

"The Historic Principles of Church Order" (G-1.0300) were adopted by the first General Assembly in 1788 in Philadelphia because of the importance of governance for Presbyterians. It has often been pointed out that the government outlined in the Constitution of the United States of America is strikingly similar to that of the Presbyterians. Both documents are based on an understanding of representative democracy, where persons elect representatives to handle the affairs of the community. As a town elects a council to handle organizational matters and disciplines those who live there, so in Presbyterian churches the congregation elects officers to handle the affairs of that church. As our nation has county, state, and a national (federal) government), so Presbyterians have sessions, presbyteries, synods, and the General Assembly. In some states, the representative body of state government is called a General Assembly, suggesting that Presbyterians may have been involved in the formation of that particular state.

Unfortunately, many Americans understand the word govern only in the political sense. They see governing as the activity of politicians. In some states, such as New Jersey where I live, politicians are considered to be largely a disreputable lot, interested only in those activities that build their egos and their holdings. Hence, an invitation to serve on a church governing body is seldom received enthusiastically!

However, our *Book of Order* holds that, "Christ gives to his Church . . . its officers. . ." (G-1.0100c). This statement acknowledges that there is more to becoming a church officer than the work of participating in a democratic process. That they have been given to the church is a truth that seems to escape many officers. Ordination to office by a governing body is a graphic reminder that a church continues through the continuous outpouring of the grace of God.

At a time when we Americans are preaching the benefits of democracy, in which people decide whom to place in positions of responsibility and where the decisions these leaders make affect many lives, it is a sad irony that subordinate institutions complain that no one is interested in governing on behalf of the greater good. To serve as an officer of the Presbyterian Church (U.S.A.) is to accept the responsibility to participate in the way a particular Presbyterian church governs itself.

Regarding who will govern in the Presbyterian Church (U.S.A.), the answer is, **"presbyters."** This noun names a group or set of people, whom we call elders. The Greek word, *presbyteros* (πρεσβψτεροσ), was used in the ancient constitution of Sparta as well as in Egyptian papyri in reference to administrative groups of various sorts. Günther Bornkamm, a New Testament scholar, notes that the reference was to function, rather than age, since persons as young as thirty are mentioned as being elders. The Septuagint, the Greek translation of the Hebrew Bible, uses the word to refer to those persons Moses calls together in Exodus 3:16, 18, and thereafter.[4]

Presbyters are elected by members (G-1.0306), which indicates that Presbyterian government is a form of democracy in the same sense that the United States form of government is democratic. That form is called representative democracy, where the people choose those persons who determine policies as well as how those policies will be implemented.

After candidates are elected, they are ordained to office. The ceremony of ordination is performed in the context of worship. In the ceremony, the biblical basis for ordination is stated, and all are reminded of the diversity of gifts in the church. A series of questions follows. The person or persons to be ordained respond by promising to conduct themselves in accord with these understandings of responsibility. Those to be ordained then kneel, and the leader of the installation, who is authorized by the governing body, invites other officers present to come and join in the "laying on of hands." Following the prayer of ordination, the previously ordained officers welcome the newly ordained.

Each officer promises to uphold nine questions, beginning with a reaffirmation of basic faith. Eight of the questions are the same for all officers. The ninth question is faithfulness in the particular office to which the person has been elected. Assent to the questions is taken seriously. Officers are accountable for their faithfulness to act according to their promises.

I find it curious that the distinctively Presbyterian word "presbyter" is so seldom used by officers or members. The simpler word appears to have disappeared from the church's vocabulary—except in the *Book of Order*. It is commonplace to refer to elders as laymen and laywomen. These terms are inappropriate, if not demeaning, for persons ordained to share in the government of a denomination.

Whenever I hear an elder say, "I'm just an elder," I shudder for two reasons. First, such a comment suggests that the individual does not take the office of elder and its obligations seriously. The eight vows that are common for both ministers and elders indicate to me that the two offices are equally significant. Second, such a comment also suggests that no one has taught the person the meaning of the vows and responsibilities.

Consequently, there is no hierarchy of persons in the Presbyterian Church (U.S.A.). The scope of responsibility differs, depending on the scope of the governing body. Some persons have gifts of leadership, which emerge in the life of a community. Each minister and each elder, whatever her or his title, has one vote in a governing body.

The parenthetical phrase, **"(elders and ministers of the Word and Sacrament, traditionally called ruling and teaching elders)"** (G-4.0301b) subtly and succinctly corrects such misunderstandings. A traditional distinction exists between **"elders and ministers of the Word and Sacrament,"** which goes back to the role of elders as **"ruling and teaching."** In 1831 Samuel Miller began his discussion of the topic with these words:

> The essential character of the officer of whom we speak is that of an *ecclesiastical ruler*. "He that ruleth, let him do it with diligence," is the summary of his appropriate functions, as laid down in scripture [*sic*]. The *teaching elder* is, indeed, also a *ruler*. In addition to this, however, he is called to preach the gospel and administer [the] sacraments. But the particular department assigned to the ruling elder is to cooperate with the pastor in spiritual inspection and government.[5]

Miller put the significance of the session for the life of a particular church in these words:

> The vote of the most humble and retiring ruling elder is of the same avail as that of his minister, so that no pastor can carry any measure unless he can obtain the concurrence of a majority of the eldership. And as the whole spiritual government of each church is committed to its bench of elders, the session is competent to regulate every concern, and to correct everything which they consider amiss in the arrangements or affairs of the church which admits of correction.[6]

Miller certainly understood the role of ruling elders to be significant for the life and work of the church. It is regrettable that so few elders today understand how critical their votes are to the mission of their church. The minister has one vote on the session, which means that the minister is always in the minority when it comes to voting. Respect for the pastor is balanced by the overwhelming voting power of the elders serving on the session.

Elders are elected by the congregation of which they are members. Many elders serve only a particular congregation, but some are commissioned to serve the larger church as commissioners to other governing bodies—presbytery, synod, and General Assembly. In these venues, the number of elders and ministers is equal. Elders also serve on all committees and commissions of these governing bodies. Thus, elders may well find themselves serving at a regional or national level.

After I was elected to the General Assembly Council in 1997, I attended several meetings before I could distinguish ministers of the Word and Sacrament from the elders. Prayers, conversation, as well as presentations to the General Assembly Council were handled with equal skill and grace by persons from both groups. I have had similar experiences in meetings of synods.

Since 1788 a basic Presbyterian principle is that "the election of the persons to the exercise of this authority [as an officer] . . . is in that society" (G-1.0306). Pastors and elders must be elected by a majority of those voting in order to have full authority in that congregation. These words require popular election of church officers, which is the foundation of *representative* democracy. Voting on most issues of church life is reserved to governing bodies.

Elders are not the only persons elected by the congregation. The congregation elects a majority of the members of the nominating committee that does the initial selection of candidates for this office. A pastor meets with this committee with authority to speak but cannot vote. Nominations from the floor are *always* invited. Representative government operates this way. The congregation also elects a pastor nominating committee when the particular church is without an installed pastor. Such committees offer recommendations to the congregation, which in turn decides whether or not to accept them. The congregation that always accepts any recommendations eventually finds itself in difficulties.

Nominating committees often find their responsibility daunting. When this committee begins with the question, "How are we going to fill all these slots?" they will find themselves struggling to roll a stone uphill, especially when the church's membership is small. Two other attitudes are preferable. One is to consider which persons are leaving active service at the end of a term and to consider what skills and gifts that person has contributed to the session. Once those have been determined, the committee can proceed with their work with focus. Another approach is to spend time discerning what gifts are needed in terms of future directions in which the church is heading and to meditate and discuss who in the church has those talents. These two approaches take seriously the affirmation in G-1.0100b, that "Christ calls the Church into being, giving it all that is necessary for its mission to the world, for its building up, and for its service to God."

The third principle turns to the way the officers are organized: **"These presbyters shall come together in governing bodies (traditionally called judicatories or courts) in regular gradation . . . " (G-4.0301c).**

This sentence is so succinct that its significance tends to be underplayed. Overlooking the significance of this principle contributes to difficulties we bemoan while looking elsewhere for the solution.

Three words bear careful scrutiny. The word **"together"** is a key word for understanding how Presbyterians govern themselves. The covenant between Presbyterians is first and foremost relational. The word **together** signals this essential relatedness, which begins with the relationships of officers in a particular church. The job descriptions for officers (see G-6.0200–.0400) clarify that they have distinct roles but work *with* one another. Officers remain disciples, servants of Jesus Christ, who is Lord of all.

The verb **"shall come"** indicates that energy and commitment are required for a governing body to discharge its responsibilities. The assumption here is that becoming part of a governing body includes a commitment to make time in one's life to fulfill the responsibilities of the governing body. Stated meetings of sessions are usually scheduled so that elders and pastors can reasonably be expected to attend. Such bodies may adopt a rule that when an elder is absent without notification for three or more times, the session may declare that elder's term vacant and ask the nominating committee to seek a replacement for the remainder of the term.

When the relational connections are broken between officers, the result is trouble until healing and reconciliation can occur.

The "killer fungus" of Presbyterian polity is a "go it alone" attitude. The *Book of Order* recognizes "the human tendency to idolatry and tyranny . . ." (G-2.0500a(4)), a theologically informed, succinct description of "go-it-alone-itus." Many painful church troubles seem to be instances where officers decided that they knew better what needed to be done than any colleagues serving in that governing body. It may be an elder who decides that her view of how the church should look on Easter Sunday is more important than how the session voted. It could be a pastor who proceeds with funding a drama program although the session has not yet authorized the program or the expenditures. We will shortly see that principle eight provides further clarity on what togetherness means in the work of a governing body.

An important term of the third principle is **"governing bodies."** This term entered the *Book of Order* in 1983. The parenthetical expression **"(traditionally called judicatories or courts)"** cryptically provides the reason for the new term through use of the word, "traditionally." Presbyterians were divided into two denominational groups at the onset of the Civil War in 1861. These two streams were reunited in 1983, when both General Assemblies met in Atlanta, Georgia, to ratify "Articles of Agreement," which had already been adopted by both General Assemblies and a majority of their respective presbyteries. Each prior denomination used a different generic name for the various bodies: the Presbyterian Church in the United States, referred to as the "southern stream," used the word **"courts,"** as in **"courts of the church."** The "northern stream," officially The United Presbyterian Church in the United States of America, preferred **"judicatories"** as the generic noun. In the negotiations, apparently, it was decided to choose a fresh generic noun, choosing **"governing bodies."** These two words have become more widely used in other settings since 1983.

The term "governing body" first emerged in the nineteenth century.[7] While the shift in usage made many uncomfortable at the time, it has become widely accepted. Ironically, while the phrase is used generally among Presbyterians, many are also uncomfortable with the notion that the business of governing bodies is to provide orderly governance. The phrase, "middle governing bodies," is sometimes used to refer to both presbyteries and synods. The phrase is not in the current *Book of Order*.

Three words used in the third principle are: **"in regular gradation."** These three simple words summarize a major dimension of Presbyterian polity. In 1797 the General Assembly articulated some radical or fundamental principles of our polity. One of the basic principles since the formation of the General Assembly in 1787, is:

> [T]hat a larger part of the Church, or a representation of it, should govern a smaller, or determine matters of controversy which arise therein; that, in like manner, a representation of the whole should govern and determine in regard to every part, and to all the parts united. . . . (G-1.0400)

The 1983 revision of the *Book of Order* reduced this to the three words, **"in regular gradation."**

Regular suggests an ordered arrangement, where governing bodies at each level have specified responsibilities in the life of the church. Unfortunately, the tendency to ascribe increased importance to those who are at higher levels of responsibility leads some to increase distrust of decisions from those governing bodies beyond the session.

A contemporary way of dealing with this issue is to speak of "more inclusive governing bodies." The rationale is that each governing body beyond the session has a geographically defined area for which it is responsible. "Presbytery" is defined in the *Book of Order* as, "a corporate expression of the church consisting of all the churches and ministers of the Word and Sacrament within a certain district" (G-11.0101). The definition of synod is "the unit of the church's life and mission which consists of not fewer than three presbyteries within a specific geographic region" (G-12.0101). The definition of the General Assembly is "the highest governing body of this church and is representative of the unity of the synods, presbyteries, sessions, and congregations of the Presbyterian Church (U.S.A.)" (G-13.0101).

A few "non-geographic presbyteries" do exist, which would seem to be an exception to the definition. A report to the General Assembly on this matter in 1993 provided the history of this exception:

> The Office of the General Assembly correctly notes that non-geographic presbyteries have been a part of our tradition since early in the nineteenth century. The formation of

Dakota Presbytery and the continuation of presbyteries within the former Welsh and German communities were considered acceptable throughout the denomination's history prior to reunion in 1983. As a nation of immigrants sensitive to the needs of Native Americans, some accommodation to culture and language differences was an acceptable way to "be Presbyterian."[8]

The provision in the *Book of Order* as it now stands (G-12.0102k) is to authorize a synod with the concurrence of existing presbyteries, to create nongeographic presbyteries in order to meet the mission needs (G-11.0103a; G-12.0102a) of identified racial ethnic or immigrant congregations; subject to the approval of the General Assembly. Such presbyteries shall be formed in compliance with the requirements of G-7.0201 and G-11.0102 and be accountable to the synod within which they were created.

The preservation of the gradation fosters order in how the church goes about its witness. This is an interesting example of how mission opportunities have affected the Presbyterian framework in the past, and continues to do so, continually adapting to emerging challenges.

Solutions that work at the level of the particular church are less effective as one ascends into the other governing bodies. The "more inclusive governing bodies" with responsibilities for larger areas with more churches and people feel more like abstract organizations, and so they require different ways of relating. One factor is the increasing diversity of persons and churches that are involved. Consequently, persons elected by presbyteries as first-time commissioners to the General Assembly find themselves overwhelmed at the amount of material they receive and the size of the committees, not to mention the points of view that differ from what they are accustomed to in their home church and presbytery.

The fourth principle lies at the heart of how Presbyterian governing bodies operate. It is an answer to, "How do Presbyterian governing bodies go about their work?" The answer is: **"Presbyters are not simply to reflect the will of the people, but rather to seek together to find and represent the will of Christ" (G-4.0301d).**

Read quickly, this principle seems to abolish rather than modify the claim that Presbyterian polity is a representative democracy. **"The will of the people"** is generally understood to be the objective of democracy. The will of twenty-first century Americans is often equated with what the latest polls show. Were that truly the case, however, we could bypass the expense and effort of elections. Few of us are interested in that approach in which a group of randomly selected persons would determine American foreign or domestic policy.

The important qualification comes in the two words, "**not simply.**" A session that utterly disregarded the will of the people would soon have a church without attending members. What members of the church express as their desire is a factor, one aspect, of the work of a governing body. Sessions care about the people in the church and take seriously what those folk say and think and believe. The people's will is definitely a factor to be considered but not the only factor.

The fourth principle recognizes that "will of the people" is expressed in many ways. Many strategies are used to influence those chosen to make policy and to determine the direction a group will take. This principle means that using strategies imported from society at large into the church are likely to have limited effect when used to try to affect governing body decisions. Demonstrating as a means of influencing decisions of a governing body indicates a lack of willingness to abide by this principle.

Some may consider the other half of the principle more daunting: "**but rather to seek together to find and represent the will of Christ.**" This indicates that what governing bodies do is essentially theological. The principal criterion is "the will of Christ." This phrase is a serious way to express that a governing body's decisions are ultimately evaluated on the basis of "What Jesus would do." Such a criterion is itself challenging, inasmuch as it includes reflection on the four gospels and the guidance of the Pauline epistles.

Many decisions that sessions make appear to be related to simple, straightforward questions: Shall the roof be replaced? Shall the sanctuary be painted? Shall the potholes in the parking lot be filled? Most of us consider these the practical matters of life. Life in the church often reveals that even those apparently simple decisions have within them aspects of faith that emerge as a body seeks to determine what to do in the specific situation. The phrase, "**to seek together to find and represent the will of Christ,**" is in a sense an indication that church decisions have to do with their witness to "the Word made flesh." Pastor Jack Haberer, a member of the Task Force on Peace, Unity, and Purity, expressed the sense of this principle when he said: "PC(USA) polity is NOT representative democracy . . . elders and presbyters don't represent the congregation or presbytery—they represent Jesus Christ."[9]

The fifth principle offers a shift from the substance of decisions to how decisions are to be made. "**Decisions shall be reached in governing bodies by vote, following opportunity for discussion, and a majority shall govern**" (G-4.0301e).

There are three parts of this principle, which cumulatively affirm democratic process. The first is the clause, "**Decisions shall be reached in governing bodies by vote**," and reaffirms the implication that reasoning together is at the heart of the deliberative process. The business of the governing body is to make **decisions**. Coming to those decisions involves work of various kinds.

Presbyterians talk a lot about committees, often not in positive ways. Committee work is a way to involve others in determining the issue involved, exploring alternative solutions, evaluating which solutions appear wisest, proposing the chosen course to the body as a whole, or presenting a recommendation to the governing body. The governing body has the responsibility of deciding whether to accept a recommendation, depending on the larger group's decision about its wisdom and value.

The next part of the principle is the phrase, "**following opportunity for discussion**." The opportunity is for discussion, not argument. Discussion—and whatever arguing might need to happen—are to be characterized by civility and a calm quest for the will of Christ and its power to reconcile persons of various points of view. Civility requires patience, taking time for persons to listen to one another in order to understand the concerns each brings to the issue.

In an impatient, "hurry-up" world, where nanoseconds determine the measure of victory, it is sometimes said that time for discussion is a luxury relevant only to an earlier time. To have opportunity for discussion requires valuing democratic process over speed and convenience. Are we willing to trade efficiency for careful deliberation? I think not, especially when the end of the decision-making process is "**to seek together to find and represent the will of Christ**" (G-4.0301d).

Such a process requires care as well as time. What do *we* think is the will of Christ for our church at this present moment? The gravity of that question should help us pause in our reflection. The only power appropriate for such discussion is found through discernment of the way that God is at work in this specific instance of our life together. A Presbyterian governing body is always standing at such a point when a question is up for a vote.

Many governing bodies have adopted the practice of using a "consent agenda" for items thought to be relatively forthright and without controversy. Any member of the body may request that an item be removed from the consent agenda, which restores it to the normal process of discussion and vote. When the moderator asks whether anyone wishes to remove an item, the opportunity for discussion is there.[10]

The final part of the fifth principle is the clause, **"and a majority shall govern."** These five words are the hallmark of democratic process.[11] *Robert's Rules of Order*'s simple definition, " '*majority*' means 'more than half . . .' "[12] is the understanding of most people. However, we must note some additional points.

First, majority generally means more than half of the persons present and voting. A tie vote means that the motion fails to garner a majority of those voting. Second, bylaws may specify that on certain specified measures, a majority exceeds a "simple majority." For example, a presbytery voting for an exception to certain requirements for ordination must do so by a three-fourths vote (G-14.0313a, b, and c). A more frequent instance happens as someone moves the previous question during debate, in order to close the debate and proceed to a vote, which requires a two-thirds majority.[13] This latter instance protects the rights of a minority perspective and establishes that most of those voting are prepared to vote on the question. This is sufficient to pass the motion. Changing the standing rules or bylaws of an organization also requires more than a simple majority, in order to protect the rights of the minority.[14]

Finally, sometimes a minority objects that the majority has erred in passing a motion that the losing side believes is contrary to the Reformed faith. Losing a vote on an issue about which one feels strongly is always painful. Sometimes persons leave the church or at least resign their office when they conclude that the majority is in error. While "freedom of conscience" is a deeply held aspect of our Presbyterian tradition (G-1.0301), it is always balanced by a commitment to corporate judgment (G-1.0302). "Majority rule" as expressed in this principle (G-1.0400) is one of the radical principles that was adopted in 1797. All the same, when one of us is in the minority on an issue about which we feel strongly, we face a crisis of where we belong. To plead "freedom of conscience" and to continue in the body as advocates for our point of view dilutes the meaning of the conscience plea. As we turn to the next principle, we will find a remedy for those who are aggrieved by a particular decision.

The sixth principle provides a key aspect for understanding Presbyterian polity, yet is arguably one of the least well understood of these nine principles: "**A higher governing body shall have the right of review and control over a lower one and shall have power to determine matters of controversy upon reference, complaint, or appeal . . ." (G-4.0301f).**

Once again, this principle restates material from G-1.0400. It describes a hierarchical ecclesiastical structure that is at the same time "**in regular gradation,**" as the third principle explained.

The first of two key elements in this principle is "**review and control.**" Those of us who are uneasy with this term are in good company. One of the major documents of our history, the so-called Swearingen Commission of 1927, noted: "It is perhaps unfortunate that this phrase 'Review and Control' is ever applied in the first sense, which makes it refer to a general power."[15] After two paragraphs of discussion, the same report concludes, "Probably the single word Review would be a better designation for the more general idea."[16]

"Review" raises concerns, especially when "control" follows it. Review has to do with "all proceedings and actions" (G-9.0407b) of church entities to the appropriate governing body (G-9.0407–.0411). The five criteria for conducting a review are specified in G-9.0409. The focus of the criteria is whether or not a governing body is following the *Constitution* in ways that are prudent and equitable. A review is analogous to an annual physical exam I schedule with my doctor. It is a way of ensuring that there are connections between the various churches and governing bodies of our denomination.

Review is significant because it serves as a reminder that we need one another. The review process may be done in various ways and with different degrees of focus, which can be "either too lax or too narrow" (G-1.0302). Review is most productive when it generates suggestions about how a group might approach its task more creatively and productively. "Control" is often understood as "correction."

The other key element in this sixth principle is, "**shall have power to determine matters of controversy upon reference, complaint, or appeal**." The surprise for many is this declaration that Presbyterians will experience controversy as one aspect of our life together. The Scotch-Irish heritage of our denomination is evident in the number of major controversies that have emerged in the almost three hundred years we have been on this continent.

One indication of this power of review is the specification of the three ways a higher governing body seeks resolution. These refer to three formal approaches, found in the "Rules of Discipline" section of the *Book of Order*. The first is "**reference**," which is the request to a higher governing body from a lower one to conduct a hearing or trial on its behalf (D-4.0101). The second means of approach is "**complaint**," the initiation of a remedial action by alleging that a governing body has either erred in a specific action, or failed to act (D-6.0202). The third means is "**appeal**," further review of a case based on one or more grounds for appeal in D-8.0105.

The words, "**shall have power to determine**," offer assurance that controversies are resolvable. It is governing bodies—rather than individuals—who are authorized to determine or resolve a controversy. The **"regular gradation"** noted earlier in the discussion of the third principle refers back to a statement from the Historic Principles of Church Government (G-1.0400): "till they be finally decided by the collected wisdom and united voice of the whole Church," which expresses a commitment that, hidden in the often tangled business of discipleship, are evidences of God's reconciling and healing love. The eighth principle will explore additional aspects of the sixth principle.

The seventh principle is, "**Presbyters are ordained only by the authority of a governing body . . .** " (G-4.0301g). Because it is so deeply embedded in Presbyterian tradition, it is tempting to consider this to be an axiom, a self-evident truth, rather than a principle. This seventh principle builds on several of the preceding principles, notably the second, third, fourth, and fifth.

Let us begin the discussion of this principle with the word "**only**." Is this word necessary? Without it, the phrase would be, "Presbyters are ordained by the authority of a governing body." Such wording is clear even with the omitted word. The significance of "**only**" is an implication of principles three and four, which express the Presbyterian commitment to corporate decision-making.

Churches with an episcopal polity ordain through the laying on of the hands of a bishop. The doctrinal basis for this is the doctrine of apostolic succession, which holds that there is a chain of authority passed on from bishop to bishop that remains unbroken since New Testament times. Since priests are the only persons eligible to become bishops, ordination in this polity requires that all priests be ordained by a bishop as well.[17] John Calvin emphatically rejected all doctrines that were not directly instituted by Jesus Christ, including this one.[18] The biblical phrase "laying on of hands" is the meaning of "ordination." Acts 6:6 and 8:18, as well as 1 Timothy 4:14, are considered bases for "ordaining" church officers.

"**A governing body**" is in this instance one authorized to ordain. Sessions are authorized "to instruct, examine, ordain, install, and welcome into common ministry elders and deacons on their election by the congregation . . . ." (G-10.0102l). Presbyteries are authorized, "to ordain, receive, dismiss, install, remove, and discipline ministers" (G-11.0103n). Neither synod nor General Assembly have authority to ordain any officers.

The final foundation for this seventh principle, noted earlier, is G-1.0306, from the first General Assembly:

> That though the character, qualifications, and authority of Church officers are laid down in the Holy Scriptures, as well as the proper method of their investiture and institution, yet the election of the persons to the exercise of this authority, in any particular society, is in that society.

Not only are persons ordained by governing bodies, they must also have been approved by God's people (G-6.0106a). This interplay also illustrates how the "regular gradation" of governing bodies is based on the will of the people of the church.

The eighth principle is the first of a pair of principles that connect previous implications: "**Ecclesiastical jurisdiction is a shared**

**power, to be exercised jointly by presbyters gathered in govern-
ing bodies** (G-4.0301h). The subject of the sentence is, "**Ecclesiastical jurisdiction.**" We are dealing with how the Presbyterian
Church (U.S.A.) governs itself.

Jurisdiction indicates a sphere within which a person is subject
to the rules and customs of that area. In New Jersey where I live, a
short drive takes me through several towns, each having its own
ordinances. For example, the speed limit often changes at the town
boundary. If I fail to adjust the speed of my car, then I am responsible to the authorities in that town for breaking the posted limit.

Ecclesiastical jurisdiction summarizes the various governing
bodies made of persons who vow in their ordination to see that
the *Constitution* of the church is upheld, together with other provisions agreed to by the relevant governing bodies. To join a
church is from one perspective to accept the **ecclesiastical jurisdiction** of a body of persons who have agreed to abide by the
way things are done in that organization.

We found earlier, while looking at the second and third principles (G-4.0301b and c) that Presbyterian officers "shall come
together in governing bodies." Now we note that ecclesiastical
jurisdiction is, "**a shared power.**" The earlier discussion of
"together" resurfaces, now as "**shared power.**" Lest the point be
misunderstood, a clause is added, "**to be exercised jointly by
presbyters gathered in governing bodies**" (G-4.0301h). The use
of the word "**jointly**" here strongly suggests that governing bodies are to work as a team, rather than become arenas for exercising personal agendas.

Another way to express the meaning of jointly might be by
using the metaphor of nets. Many sorts of nets are available, but
the word conveys an object with fibrous material stretched out
thinly into convergent points separating clear spaces. The points
are the loci where threads come together. "Governing bodies" are
the convergence zones of the Presbyterian Church. There are
numerous connections between these groups, yet there is also an
order to the total entity. The Apostle Paul suggested another
metaphor for this relationship when he proposed that the particular churches of his time should understand themselves to be the
body of Christ (1 Cor. 12, Eph. 4).

The sphere of "**shared power**" is explicitly outlined in the
chapter of the *Book of Order* that deals with that level of governing

body (G-10.0000 for the session, G-11.0000 for the presbytery, G-12.0000 for the synod, and G-13.0000 for the General Assembly). Each of these chapters sets forth the specific responsibilities for which that level of governing body is responsible.

The ninth and final principle crowns the set: "**Governing bodies possess whatever administrative authority is necessary to give effect to duties and powers assigned by the Constitution of the church**" (G-4.0301i). This final principle was added to the *Book of Order* in 1987. The overture requesting this addition (153–85,) came from the Presbytery of New Covenant. It cited a provision in the *Book of Church Order* of the former Presbyterian Church in the United States. The rationale for the proposed addition also included the comment:

> The Constitution assigns a responsibility or duty to a particular governing body because it is more appropriate to that body, and it can be fulfilled best by the abilities inherent in that body to which the duty or responsibility is assigned. Such being the situation, that particular governing body will ordinarily know what administrative procedures will be most helpful.[19]

The vote on this overture was 165 presbyteries in favor, 11 against, and no abstentions.[20] Similar language is found in *The Constitution of the United States*.[21]

Eight years later, this principle was cited in the decision of the Permanent Judicial Commission regarding a 1992 dispute in the Alamance Presbyterian Church, Greensboro, North Carolina, regarding the election process of members of an associate pastor nominating committee. None of the twenty-three alleged errors in the final case were sustained. Rephrasing the heart of the principle, "**whatever administrative authority is necessary . . . ,**" the Permanent Judicial Commission commented: "The *Book of Order* is not a straitjacket that prevents a governing body from exercising its powers in a reasonable way so as to carry out its basic functions and duties with efficiency to avoid a waste of time of its members (*Book of Order*, G-4.0301i)."[22] This principle holds a key to our denomination, offering latitude in the way the church fulfills its mission within the framework of our *Constitution*. Our *Book of Confessions* sketches the outlines of our Christian faith. Our *Book of Order* defines duties and responsibilities, as well as the roles of members and officers. As long as these provisions are respected, how they are implemented and maintained is the responsibility of the governing bodies directly involved.

Latitude is not a word many associate with the *Book of Order*. This final principle affirms that how decisions of a governing body become effective depends on how the governing body understands the situation at hand. As noted earlier, there is often more than one way to be Presbyterian within the polity of our church. Churches vary according to size, history, funding, community, region, and a host of other dimensions. How sessions understand mission depends on their particular point of view and concerns, and for this reason there is a range of understanding across the Presbyterian Church U.S.A. This latitude is specifically addressed in a lengthy paragraph (G-9.0901), which begins: "Within this Constitution, it has been assumed that the governing bodies beyond the session will delegate particular aspects of their task to councils, commissions, and committees." The final sentence in this paragraph reinforces the sentiment: "Reference to such agencies . . . is not intended to limit the governing bodies to these structures but to describe those which will expedite the mutual work of the whole church" (G-9.0901).

This principle declares that governing bodies have immense latitude to determine how to go about the mission for which they are responsible. Governing bodies above the session have some structurally required committees listed in G-9.0902. Sessions, which are the most numerous of the governing bodies, have **no** required committees.

Some may say that "being Presbyterian" is synonymous with "serving on committees." To assume that "everyone knows what a committee is" is dangerous. *Robert's Rules of Order* defines a committee in its function in parliamentary law as "a body of one or more persons, elected or appointed by (or by the direction of) an assembly or society, to consider, investigate, or take action on certain matters or subjects, or to do all of these things."[23] The definition in the *Book of Order* (G-9.0501a) is more precise:

> A committee is appointed either to study and recommend appropriate action or to carry out directions or decisions already made by a governing body. It shall make a full report to the governing body that created it, and its recommendations shall require action by the governing body.

Those serving on governing body committees need to clarify whether their task is to "study and recommend" or to "carry out directions." Sometimes committees fail to acknowledge that a committee's report "**require[s] action by the governing body.**" A committee recommendation is a suggested course of action until the governing body acts.

This final principle has particular significance for every session. When the session is small, a committee may consist of one elder, with others from the congregation approved by the session. Committee decisions are exercises in stewardship of time of the elders and members, the decisions depend upon the skills of the membership and the scope of the ministry of the church. The foundation for this is a sense of how the church will be faithful in its mission and responsible to the denomination.

As a temporary moderator of session,[24] I have witnessed many discussions focused on whether or not the session had the authority to make certain decisions. The answer is always "yes," if what needs to be done relates to one of the "responsibilities and powers" listed in G-10.0102.

This brings us to the end of the nine principles of Presbyterian polity. We will consider the remaining three paragraphs of G-4.0302–.0304 in the next chapter.

Notes

1. J. Aspinwall Hodge, *What Is Presbyterian Law?* (Philadelphia: Presbyterian Board of Publication and Sabbath School Work, 1907), p. 30. A footnote indicates that this is taken from *Presbyterian Digest*, p. 119. No further identification of this source is given.
2. Session, Central Church v. Presbytery of Long Island, Remedial Case 204–205, 1992, 11.050. Reference is to the *Minutes of the General Assembly*, 1992, p. 179.
3. Ibid.
4. Günther Bornkamm, "πρεσβψτεροσ." in Gerhard Friedrich, ed., *Theological Dictionary of the New Testament*, vol. VI (Grand Rapids: Wm. B. Eerdmans Publishing, 1968), p. 653.
5. Samuel Miller, *The Ruling Elder*, 2nd Edition (Dallas: Presbyterian Heritage Publications, 1994) p. 11. The 45-page pamphlet is "based upon an *An Essay, on the Warrant, Nature and Duties of the Office of the Ruling Elder, in the Presbyterian Church* (New York: Jonathan Leavitt; (Boston: Crocker and Brewster, 1831) front matter, unnumbered page. The quote is from Romans 12:8.
6. Ibid., p. 15. Masculine pronouns are in the original text and left in for historical accuracy.

7. *Shorter Oxford English Dictionary on Historical Principles,* 5th ed., vol. 1 (Oxford: Oxford University Press, 2002), p. 1131.

8. *Minutes of the 213th General Assembly* (2001), p. 109.

9. Note #8533 from *PCUSA News to Presbynews,* 10/16/04.

10. The authoritative presentation of this is called the "consent calendar," discussed in *Robert's Rules of Order, Newly Revised,* 10th ed., (Cambridge: Perseus Publishing, 2000), pp. 349–50. For the role of *Robert's,* see also G-7.0302c regarding meetings of congregations and G-9.0302 for governing bodies, committees, and commissions.

11. See Ibid., pp. xlvii, 4, and 387–88.

12. Ibid., p. 387.

13. Ibid., p. 192.

14. In the spring of 2005, the majority leader of the United States Senate announced that a simple majority of the Senate could change a rule regarding the closing of debate, that the majority of the senators could change the rules of the body. In the heated debate that followed, there was virtually no mention from either side that this attempt was against *Robert's* and the principle of protecting the right of a minority.

15. "PCUSA, 1927, pp. 56–86, Report of the Special Commission of 1925." From *The Annotated Book of Order, Software Edition,* 2003–2004.

16. Ibid.

17. The ordination of a bishop is a separate rite in Episcopal churches.

18. *Calvin: Institutes of the Christian Religion,* vol. XXI of *The Library of Christian Classics,* ed. John T. McNeill, trans. Ford Lewis Battles (Philadelphia: The Westminster Press, 1960), pp. 1196–1197.

19. *Minutes of the 198th General Assembly (1986). Part I, Journal* (New York, NY and Atlanta, GA: Office of the General Assembly), p. 772.

20. *Minutes of the 199th General Assembly (1987). Part I, Journal* (New York, NY and Atlanta, GA: Office of the General Assembly), p. 30.

21. Article 1, Section 8, concludes with "To make all Laws which shall be necessary and proper carrying into Execution the foregoing Powers, and all other Powers vested by this Constitution in the Government of the United States, or in any Department or Officer thereof." From Forrest MacDonald, *Novus Ordo Seclorum: The Intellectual Origins of the Constitution* (Lawrence, KS: University Press of Kansas, 1985), p. 304. I discovered this connection while reading Carol Belkin, *A Brilliant Solution: Inventing the American Constitution* (New York: A Harvest Book, Harcourt, Inc., 2002).

22. *Minutes of the 207th General Assembly (1995). Part I, Journal* (Louisville: Office of the General Assembly), p. 118.

23. *Robert's Rules of Order,* 10th ed., pp. 417—472.

24. Temporary moderators of session are assigned by a presbytery (G-10.0103b).

FOUR

Declaratory Principles

The three concluding paragraphs of G-4.0300 shift from particular axioms of Presbyterian polity to three declaratory paragraphs more general in tone, offering principles of a different sort from the nine discussed in G-4.0301. These three statements, G-4.0302–.0304, provide important background describing the conditions in which the previous nine principles of G-4.0301 function at their best.

Each of the principles that we will explore in this chapter stands on its own while at the same time contributing to a larger whole by describing additional layers of the context. As we take these next three steps, we move toward a more comprehensive understanding of how the Presbyterian system is intended to operate. The convictions presented in the earlier sections of G-4.0000 will culminate in the last paragraph, G-4.0403.

In chapter four we looked at the unity of the church as a theological concept. We saw that the principles of polity affirm that "The particular churches of the Presbyterian Church (U.S.A.) wherever they are, taken collectively, constitute one church" (G-4.0301a). The first of these declaratory principles lays out the nature of Presbyterian unity: "**The nature of Presbyterian order is such that it shares power and responsibility. The system of governing bodies, whether they have authority over one or many churches, sustains such mutual relationships within the structures as to express the unity of the church" (G-4.0302).**

By rearranging some words in this provision, we could say that Presbyterian polity is a system of responsible power-sharing governing bodies. The *Book of Order* specifies which responsibilities belong to which governing bodies in chapters X through XIII. Each of these chapters has a section that defines the area to be governed and then introduces the itemized list with the words, **"It, therefore, has the responsibility and power . . . "** **(G-10.0102, 11.0103, 12.0102, and 13.0103).**

"Shares" is a key word in understanding the intent of G-4.0302, as well as the dynamic of the Presbyterian system. Most of us learn how to share during our preschool years, but sharing seems to become more difficult as we develop a sense of ownership. "Mine" overpowers "ours" so easily. Betrayals of trust engender suspicion that "others" no longer are playing fair, setting up the dynamics of suspicion that erode trust and community.

The story of the West Side Presbyterian Church of Ridgewood, New Jersey, illustrates how sharing operates. West Side is the largest church in Palisades Presbytery, with nearly 1500 members. West Side has supported the mission of our denomination at each level for years. When the church's sanctuary burned on January 8, 2002, one of the first responses came in the form of a check from Presbyterian Disaster Assistance. The impact of this expression of support and concern demonstrated that sharing is never a one-way street.

The **"power"** indicated in this principle is defined in the seventh Historic Principle (G-1.0307): "all Church power, whether exercised by the body in general or in the way of representation by delegated authority, is only ministerial and declarative." The scriptural basis for this statement is Acts 15:1–32, where the Council of Jerusalem is called to settle the dispute in Antioch about Paul and Barnabas baptizing Gentiles without requiring that they be circumcised. Once the council had worked out a response, they sent a letter and two more representatives to Antioch to explain the decision.

Any **power** the church has comes from Jesus Christ, to whom all power "has been given" (Mat. 28:18, G-1.0100a). Ordained officers vow to "fulfill [their] office in obedience to Jesus Christ"(G–14.0207d).[1] Consequently, ordination vows confer ministerial authority from the Lord of the church. Making such a vow obliges the person to be a good steward of such gifts as God has provided. Breaking these vows constitutes an offense against both the church and the church's Lord.

With the gift of power comes "**responsibility,**" another dimension of sharing. While Presbyterians realize that we all are personally accountable for our actions, our polity also means that we answer to one another for how we behave. We have "general administrative review" (G-9.0407), which establishes a system of having our work reviewed by others. Such review begins with the congregation: "The congregation of a particular church and the committees, bodies, and organizations of that church shall report annually all proceedings and actions to the session, which shall review and summarize them and incorporate the summary in its minutes" (G-9.0407a).

A 1997 General Assembly statement defined a reviewable entity: "It is any individual or group which arises within the membership that affects theological instruction, spiritual development, mission programs, raises money, uses property, or purports in any way to represent the congregation to the public."[2] Such review of records continues throughout the governing body system. The criteria for these reviews are listed in G-9.0409. The purpose of review is to correct errors in recording, to remedy instances of lack of prudence or equity, to address failure to follow the *Constitution*, and to be faithful to the church's mission and obedient to "lawful injunctions of a higher governing body" (G-9.0409a(5)).

Other forms of correction may be used when "general administrative review" is not adequate. One of these is "special administrative review" (G-9.0408), which is to be used in those instances where regular review is inadequate. When this fails, there is also a formal "remedial" process to correct situations in which governing bodies either act erroneously or fail to act (D-2.0202). The steps in each of these processes are found in D-6.0000—8.0000.

An important and generally overlooked phrase appears as the subject of the next sentence of G-4.0302: "**The system of governing bodies . . .**" We Presbyterians tend to refer to our structure more often than to our system. This tendency skews our perception, putting the focus on the pieces rather than the relationships. We could help ourselves by substituting "our Presbyterian system" for "our Presbyterian structure." Such a change would have the benefit of the biblical metaphor of the church as the body of Christ, central to G-1.0100 as well as other places in our *Constitution*.

The systems perspective enhances our sense of belonging to one another as one church. Such a point of view further emphasizes the dynamic character of the church as an arena for God's Holy Spirit to be continually at work. When we recall the traditional definition of the church as, "'The church reformed, always reforming' according to the Word of God and the call of the Spirit" (G-2.0200), we see the possibilities of understanding our denomination as a system.

The next phrase, "**whether they have authority over one or many churches**," is significant for an understanding of our system of government. Higher governing bodies are more inclusive in the sense that their authority is broader, "covering more territory." This phrase directly addresses the common tendency of deference to "more inclusive governing bodies," a deference that often is coupled with suspicion and mistrust of them. At this point, the significance of our Presbyterian system is highlighted, leading us to the concluding phrase.

The climax of this paragraph comes in the final phrase: "**sustains such mutual relationships within the structures as to express the unity of the church**" (G4.0302). The key to the Presbyterian way of being church in a nutshell has to do with "**such mutual relationships**." Mutuality is not imposed in our system. Rather, mutuality comes through the dynamic interplay of all the governing bodies.

We are familiar in our national life with the notion of a balance of powers among the three branches of government: executive, legislative, and judicial. Ways in which that balancing occurs in the day-to-day operation of government is a primary concern of the media most days—notice the subject of so many radio and television talk shows. Someone is usually upset at something that is or is not done by another branch of government, or the other party. Over time, however, the balance continues to work, much to the distress of those who have a proposal to improve on our basic constitutional structure. Our history has shown us that seldom do these proposals rise to the level of an amendment to our *Constitution*.

The Presbyterian Church (U.S.A.) is much smaller than our nation and professes obedience to the Lord of the Church, Jesus Christ. Among the different ways to organize church life, our Presbyterian system recognizes that, while we will have our differences, we also share our commitment to Jesus Christ (G-1.0100; G-2.0000).[3]

Our life together as Presbyterians is not only a matter of the interconnections of our system. It is even more a response to the call "**to express the unity of the church**" (G-4.0302). Once more, as we have seen repeatedly, this principle challenges us to be vigilant that "how" we behave with one another is at least as important as the "what" in our *Book of Order*. The way we live with one another is more valuable as the order that is the subject of the *Book of Order*. The theological basis for such an expression isin G-1.0100c: "**Christ gives to his Church . . . its unity and mission. . . .**" Unity is an expression of Christian discipleship.

The second of the three declaratory principles in G-4.0300 again presents a paradox to be balanced: "**The Presbyterian system of government calls for continuity with and faithfulness to the heritage which lies behind the contemporary church. It calls equally for openness and faithfulness to the renewing activity of the God of history.**"

This principle raises the issue: "What constitutes "**the heritage which lies behind the contemporary church?**" Most of us understand our heritage as "the way we've always done things in our church." Since heritage is much more than personal recollections and impressions, comments such as "Presbyterians have always . . ." or "Presbyterians have never . . ." are frequently incorrect in terms of our history.[4]

An assignment I gave when teaching seminarians an introduction to our history was to create conversations between Presbyterians regarding a current issue in church life. Each conversation was to be between two people, and one conversation had to be about an issue from the eighteenth, mid-nineteenth, or early twentieth century, as well as a contemporary issue. The assignment offered the students an opportunity to choose their specific topics. It produced engaging essays and demonstrated that our history has continued to deal with persisting issues throughout decades and even centuries.[5]

My personal introduction to the richness and complexity of Presbyterian history was the preparation of an independent study paper at the College of Wooster in 1954–55. At that time, the Synod of Ohio archive was stored at the college. I was permitted to examine these records for a paper, titled "Ohio Presbyterians and Slavery: 1830–1860."[6] My major conclusion from the study was that "the content of the various resolutions, memorials, and judgements display a wide range of feeling concerning that issue [slavery]."[7] Since then, this conclusion has been borne out in the Presbyterian history I have read.

The Presbyterian Historical Society, located in Philadelphia, Pennsylvania, and Montreat, North Carolina, founded in 1852, reflects our commitment to history. The Society archives records of churches and governing bodies. An electronic catalog provides information on over 75,000 books, periodicals, and other archival materials.[8] The 2005 budget approved by the General Assembly was slightly less than $2.1 million dollars.[9] The Society also publishes a quarterly *Journal of Presbyterian History*. Presbyterian Heritage Sunday in May is another way the Historical Society reminds us of the importance of our heritage.

The Book of Confessions offers documents tracing the history of doctrine of the Presbyterian Church (U.S.A.). The purpose of our *Book of Confessions* is summarized in G-2.0100a: "In these confessional statements the church declares to its members and to the world who/and what it is,/what it believes,/what it resolves to do." This is further evidence of the role that heritage plays in the Presbyterian Church.

A summary of the Presbyterian theological **heritage** is offered in G-2.0000, "The Church and Its Confessions." This chapter outlines the textual and confessional basis for our core beliefs. Of course, the cornerstone of our **heritage** is Scripture, as indicated in G-2.0200: "These confessional statements are subordinate standards in the church, subject to the authority of Jesus Christ, the Word of God, as the Scriptures bear witness to him. While confessional standards are subordinate to the Scriptures, they are, nonetheless, standards."

The Westminster Confession of Faith offers a way of to understand the way in which the "the Scriptures bear witness to him." The section titled "Of the Holy Scripture" begins by affirming that "the whole counsel of God"[10] is set forth in Scripture. It goes on to remind us that the Bible is a complex book to be understood in its fullness. The tendency to cite a verse and then to endow it with an aura of unimpeachable authority is to risk taking that verse out of context and, thus, to be less than faithful stewards of the Word of God.

The government of our church calls for "**continuity with and faithfulness to the heritage**" (G-4.40303). The principle suggests that heritage is a foundation of the church, and it is to be taken seriously, to be studied as an indication of how people of faith in the past resolved the puzzles and paradoxes of the Christian life. At the same time it is not to be taken either so seriously that the tradition strangles the present and the future or so loosely that the difficult lessons of the past are neglected.

The phrase, "**heritage which lies behind the contemporary church**," affirms the significance of becoming familiar with our heritage for contemporary witness. This heritage may be somewhat hidden, and we might neglect it in our busyness. Such amnesia is unfortunate, in that we tend to lose sight of the humanness of the church. Although yesterday's solutions to recurring problems may not be appropriate in today's world, awareness that issues persist frees us from the tendency to see emerging difficulties as unprecedented. While heritage plays a role in how Presbyterians do their work, there is a balancing factor: "**It** [the Presbyterian system of government] **calls equally for openness and faithfulness to the renewing activity of the God of history**" (G-4.0303), another rephrasing of "'The church reformed, always reforming,' according to the Word of God and the call of the Spirit"(G-2.0200).

The adverb "**equally**" stands out in this sentence. "Continuity and faithfulness to the heritage" and "openness and faithfulness to the renewing activity in the God of history" demand equal time on the church's agenda. I find myself caught up short by this word, and I am alerted to pay careful attention to what follows. The use of the word **equally** suggests that such balance has not always been the case, and it also calls us to exercise care that balance between these two sides of the paradox is maintained as much as possible. This sentence could serve as a contemporary way of expressing Paul's reminder to the Church in Corinth: "[W]e have this treasure in clay jars" (2 Cor. 4:7).

We have likely been better at **faithfulness** than at **openness**. Some Presbyterians consider **openness** a threat to **faithfulness**. To address this, we must ask what it is to which we are to be open and faithful. This is not a new kind of question for American Presbyterians. As early as 1817, shortly after the departure of what became the Cumberland Presbyterian Church, the General Assembly stated in a Pastoral Letter:

"That differences of opinion, acknowledged on all hands to be of the minor class, may and ought to be tolerated among those who are agreed in great and leading views of divine truth, is a principle on which the godly have so long and so generally acted, that it seems unnecessary, at the present day, to seek arguments for its support. . . . Surely, those who can come together on the great principles of our public standards, however they may disagree on non-essential points, ought not to separate, or to indulge in bitterness or prejudice against each other."[11]

On the eve of reuniting the Old School and New School branches (1867), Henry Boynton Smith suggested the concept of "allowable differences":

"These allowable differences must, of course, be such as do not impair the integrity of the system, as distinguished from Lutheranism, Arminianism, Pelagianism, etc., nor vitiate any one of the doctrines that make up the system. But within these limits, there have been, and still are, very considerable diversities."[12]

The focus of G-4.0303 is on "**the renewing activity of the God of history**." As noted earlier, the Latin motto of the reformation is, "Ecclesia reformata, simper reformanda, the church reformed, ever reforming." The *Book of Order* makes explicit that the activity of reformation is "according to the Word of God and the call of the Spirit" (G-2.0200). On this basis, the answer to the question posed (to what do we need to remain open?), is "**the renewing activity of the God of history.**" As James Russell Lowell wrote in his 1845 hymn:

New occasions teach new duties,
Time makes ancient good uncouth;
They must upward still and onward,
Who would keep abreast of truth.[13]

The answer leads us to ask another question: "**How do we recognize God's renewing activity?**" The simple answer "because we read about it in the Bible" is correct in the same sense that one believes that everyone in Texas or New York City knows your friend who came from there. Simple answers are analogous to chemical litmus tests in that they are correct only in a general sense. However, life and history present daily specificities that are difficult to fit into such general statements. So too does Scripture provide particular ways in which God has acted in history.

I recognize God's renewing activity "by considering how God has acted in the past, beginning with creation." A brief and helpful presentation of God's activity as told in the Bible is offered in G-3.0100.[14] Unpredictability of what God will do and how God will act are distinguishing hallmarks of God's activity (Isa. 55:8–9, Rom. 11:33), as well as God's delight and joy in the process.

Discerning what God is doing in history is a daunting task, not to be undertaken carelessly. Voices always proclaim what it is that God is doing, not all of which can be correct. Reading any of the Old Testament prophets provides ample evidence of the prevalent skepticism regarding any who make claims to such knowledge. It is important to continue to proclaim the hope in Christ begun on Easter and continuing.

The challenge is how to be open to God at work in history, without being gullible. This second principle offers yet again the challenge to keep a paradox before us, choosing carefully and together, as we seek to be faithful disciples.

The third and final declaratory principle is titled "Ecumenical Awareness." G-4.0304 states: **"This form of government is established in the light of Scripture to give order to this church but is not regarded as essential to the existence of the Church of Jesus Christ nor to be required of all Christians."** The final "principle as balancing act" builds on the earlier emphasis on openness. It may come as a surprise that at the conclusion, the crown of all the "Principles of Presbyterian Government," we find such humility. While Presbyterians are firm in our understanding and commitment to our polity, we also understand that openness to what God is doing leads to the affirmation that what we are working out is not the last word for all Christians.

We have already seen in chapter three that Presbyterians are "willing to seek and to maintain communion and community with all other branches of the one, catholic Church (G-15.0000)" (G-4.0203). This sense of fellowship is deep in our Presbyterian heritage. Historian Janet G. Macgregor concluded her 1926 study of Scottish Presbyterian polity by commenting:

In contrast with the simple Scriptural origin claimed for the Scottish reformed polity, stands the highly composite origin, of which internal evidence has been found in the forms of the constitution itself. There is evidence of the formative elements of Lambert's Hessian constitution, of the Swiss, and especially of the Genevan reformation, of the foreign churches of a'Lasco and of Pullain in England, with some slight influence of the Edwardian Church of England itself, and of close study of the new French ecclesiastical polity.[15]

This conclusion indicates that our roots as Presbyterians extend into many traditions. To be true to our roots, we must have an ecumenical spirit.

Notes

1. The vow for ministers specifies, "Will you be a minister of the Word and Sacrament . . . ?" which is included in the more generic vow cited.
2. *Minutes of the 209th General Assembly, 1997, Part I, Journal* (Louisville: Office of the General Assembly, 1997), p. 186.
3. Further discussion of the role of our history comes in the next section, where we explore our historical awareness.
4. Comments such as these occur in "Letters to the Editor" in various Presbyterian-related periodicals as expressions of personal distress, rather than accurate reflections of our heritage.
5. The suggestion that the persisting issues are present in the "Historic Principles of Church Order" (G-1.0300) is explored in detail in my *History and Theology in the Book of Order: Blood on Every Page* (Louisville: Witherspoon Press, 1999).
6. The full title is, "Ohio Presbyterians and Slavery, 1830–1860: A documentary history of the social thought of religious institutions on a serious secular problem." The original is in the library of the College of Wooster.
7. Ibid., p. 94.
8. Web site at www.history.pcusa.org.
9. *Minutes of the 216th General Assembly (2004), Part I, Journal* (Louisville: Office of the General Assembly, 2004) p. 195.
10. The Westminster Confession of Faith, *The Book of Confessions*, 6.006.
11. *Minutes of the General Assembly, 1817*, pp. 653–656. Cited in footnote 46 of S. Donald Fortson, III, "New School Calvinism and the Presbyterian Creed," *The Journal of Presbyterian History*, 82, no. 4 (Winter 2004): 242.

12. Ibid., p. 237. This quotation is from H. B. Smith, "Presbyterian Reunion," in *American Presbyterian and Theological Review V* (October 1867),642–665.
13. "Once to Every Man and Nation," #221, *The Hymnal for Youth* (Philadelphia: The Westminster Press, 1941).
14. For a discussion and analysis of G-3.0100, see my book, *Mission Symphony: Notes for the Third Millennium* (Louisville: The Witherspoon Press, 2004), pp. 10–29.
15. Janet G. MacGregor, *The Scottish Presbyterian Polity: A Study of Its Origins in the Sixteenth Century* (Edinburgh: Oliver and Boyd, 1926), p. 132.

FIVE

Mix and Match

D iversity is rooted in Scripture, according to Samuel Wells, an
Anglican priest. He contends that not one single book of the
Bible tells the whole of God's story; rather, each one is necessary
for the complete rendering of who God is. He asserts:

> No single church or denomination can claim to incorporate
> every aspect of God's purposes. Each has a different blend
> of faithfulness, discipline, suffering, courage and wisdom.
> But diversity and disunity are not the same thing. Diversity
> is a sign of health in the church, so long as it mirrors the
> diversity of scripture. But when the church believes it can
> read the Bible without the eyes and ears of some of these
> diverse elements, its diversity becomes disunity, and its
> ability to hear God's word is seriously impoverished.[1]

Closer to our community of faith, one of the recurrent themes
of an article in the Princeton seminary magazine *InSpire,* titled
"What would you like to tell Professor Torrance about Princeton
Seminary?," "was the need to help the Presbyterian Church USA
to deal effectively with diversity."[2]

You may ask, "Why does this chapter about G-4.0400 begin
with quotes from a British Anglican priest and American seminarians?" One reason is to provide illustrations of the Presbyterian commitment to the international Christian community. The
other reason is to demonstrate how the chapter on "Diversity
and Inclusiveness," which was inserted at the time of the 1983
reunion, is consistent with the convictions of those outside the
Presbyterian circle.

65

G-4.0401 opens the final section of Chapter IV with two sentences: one a statement of conviction; the other its implications for the church. The provision first declares that: "**The church in its witness to the uniqueness of the Christian faith is called to mission and must be responsive to diversity in both the church and the world.**"

The form and force of this sentence echoes G-3.0401, which declares four times that "the Church is called to a new openness." The words "**witness to the uniqueness of the Christian faith**" are significant because they presuppose that openness is an essential aspect of our faith in Christ. Presbyterians understand openness to derive from biblical material, including Jesus' conversation with the woman at the well (John 4:7–30) and the Parable of the Good Samaritan (Luke 10:29–37), two Scripture passages in which Jesus' concern for others transcends religious and cultural differences. Thus, Christian attention to diversity is not rooted in politics or sociology or any other source.

Diversity is the result of Pentecost, as the good news preached by the disciples was heard in the many languages of those present from around the known world (Acts 2:8–11). Because of the way the issue about the necessity of non–Jews converting to Christianity to be circumcised was presented, the way the discussion proceeded, and finally the decision to send a letter and a delegation to the affected churches, many consider Acts 15 to be a description of the first presbytery (or synod) meeting! The focus was Paul's compliance with an earlier interpretation of Jesus' message and the way Paul and others of his persuasion should proceed in the future. This passage exemplifies how "**openness to diversity**" is related to the "**uniqueness of the Christian faith.**"

> The Second Helvetic Confession (1561) comments on "diversity": And, therefore, we read in the ancient writers that there was a manifold diversity of rites, but that they were free, and no one ever thought that the unity of the Church was thereby dissolved. So we teach that the true harmony of the Church consists in doctrines and in the true and harmonious preaching of the Gospel of Christ, and in rites that have been expressly delivered by the Lord.[3]

This culmination of the sentence is "**must be responsive to diversity. . . .**" The imperative "**must**" calls us to appropriate responses to what the New Testament teaches. As the Brief

Statement of Faith puts it, celebrating the church's mission of reconciliation:

In a broken and fearful world
the Spirit gives us courage
to pray without ceasing,
to witness among all peoples to Christ as Lord and Savior,
to unmask idolatries in Church and culture,
to hear the voices of peoples long silenced,
and to work with others for justice, freedom, and peace.[4]

This comment suggests that diversity has been a fact of life for the church from its earliest days. The text of 1 Corinthians 12 teaches us that the Apostle Paul recognized a "diversity of gifts" within the one body of Christ.

As our world changes, the faithful continually choose an appropriate response to those changes. The reason that God has given us spiritual treasure is "in order to show that the supreme power belongs to God, not to us" (2 Cor. 4:7).[5] The issue is not whether we will respond to diversity but how. Responsiveness is an essential characteristic for learning. From our earliest times in Scotland, Presbyterians have been deeply committed to fostering education, shown in our founding and sustaining schools, colleges, universities, and seminaries. The motto of the College of Wooster expresses the scope and purpose of openness in its motto, "*Scientia et religio ex uno fonte*," meaning, "Science and religion from the same source."[6] Many Presbyterian colleges now share this position.[7]

Education becomes indoctrination when avenues of learning are closed off. When we are unable to learn from change, our opinions about the world often harden, and the power that we have becomes brittle. We may have less ability to function effectively in the face of change, and disputes with other groups, who regard truth differently than we, multiply. The same holds for people and groups that choose to tune out anything that contradicts their opinions. Railing at diversity suggests nostalgia for a bygone time or deafness to change in our situation as a church. Such suspicion tends to lead to the ghettoization of the church.

Setri Nyomi, general secretary of the World Alliance of Reformed Churches, addresses the situation of the contemporary church in a way consistent with Chapter IV of our *Book of Order*:

Can Christians today be inspired to express a living faith which address [sic] the challenges of our days? . . . We are indeed in a very challenging era. What is called for is not easy answers, but the readiness to struggle with the resources which those who have gone before us have left as a legacy of living faith for their times. The living faith, which is relevant for our days, continues to stand on the wisdom attributed to Karl Barth—holding the Bible in one hand, and newspapers in the other.[8]

Nyomi's statement prepares us for the next phrase, **"in both the church and the world."** This phrase reminds us that while we wonder how to "sing the Lord's song/in a foreign land" (Ps. 137:4), it is to this strange country of the twenty-first century to which we must bear witness. A recent study of Colossians suggests that we remix our message, understanding that "remixing is a matter of 'revoicing,' allowing the original song to be sung again in a contemporary context that is culturally and aesthetically different. Such remixing honors and respects the integrity and brilliance of the original piece while helping it to be heard anew in the ears and lives of people with different cultural sensibilities."[9] Remixing, a term used in contemporary music, in the context of the church means taking a serious and critical look at how people are changing in matters of taste and language and discerning a fresh way to present the message so that it can be heard by those whose perceptions differ from those for whom it was originally written.

Maintaining the balance, discerning how to remix the message, remains challenging. For example, while it was often said that the Revolutionary War was a Presbyterian rebellion, not all Presbyterians were eager to become involved or to support the colonial cause. We can never escape change **"in both the church and the world,"** even as we witness to the eternal God, "with whom there is no variation or shadow due to change" (James 1:17).

Responding to diversity and the change it usually implies can range from stubborn denial to uncritical assimilation. Neither extreme response has been characteristic of American Presbyterians, although both tendencies have periodically arisen and claimed to represent the essential core of our fellowship. The process of response at best is slow and deliberate, rooted in the conviction that resolution comes when, "appeals . . . [are] finally decided by the collected wisdom and united voice of the whole Church" (G-1.0400).[10]

The second sentence in G-4.0401 begins with **"thus,"** a word that alerts us that behavioral implications of the preceding discussion of diversity are about to appear. We are about to find out what is involved in a Presbyterian response to diversity: **"Thus the fellowship of Christians as it gathers for worship and orders its corporate life will display a rich variety of form, practice, language, program, nurture, and service to suit culture and need."**

The designated scope of this sentence is the fellowship that is broader than that of official church members. This reference includes all people gathered in a particular church for any worship service.

The expected consequence of diversity is that the fellowship **"will display a rich variety . . . ."** "Variety" is another word for diversity. As a nationwide denomination, it is not surprising that there is in fact variety in the Presbyterian fellowship. The question is, "What counts as a **'rich'** variety?"

The six modes in which variety in the life of the Presbyterian Church (U.S.A.) are to be expressed are explained below.

Form. The *Book of Order*'s "Directory for Worship" provides "principles" for ordering worship (W–3.1000), noting: "The Church has always experienced a tension between form and freedom in worship" as it aims toward "worship which is orderly yet spontaneous . . . " (W-3.1002a). The "Form of Government" indicates responsibilities for each of the governing bodies in corporate life (G-10.0103, for example).

Practice. How we Presbyterians go about worship and our life together varies widely from church to church. As Pastor Nominating Committees seek candidates, or as members visit other Presbyterian churches, the variety of practices becomes evident as they observe how their cousins go about being church, sometimes to their dismay. Neighboring presbyteries often have bylaws or standing rules—as well as meetings—that are significantly different.

Language. Currently, Presbyterian immigrants to the United States of America have the opportunity to spread the gospel in numerous languages. The General Assembly now provides simultaneous translation of its plenary proceedings, so all commissioners can participate in the deliberations. A helpful discussion of Authentic and Appropriate Language is found in the Directory for Worship (W-1.2005) as is a discussion on Inclusive Language (W-1.2006).

Programs. G-10.0102c grants the session of every Presbyterian church the responsibility "to lead the congregation in participation in the mission of the whole Church in the world, in accordance with G-3.0000." One guide for program is the annual "Presbyterian Program Calendar," listing suggestions for sessions as they plan their year's work. The variety of sizes and situations of churches affects how many and what sort of programs they will implement as they respond to God's call to mission in their specific situation.

Nurture. Nurture is "a process of bringing [believers and their children] to full maturity in Jesus Christ" (W-6.1003). A list of some of the ways in which nurture is manifest in the church follows (W-6.2000), including practical guidance for building up the body of Christ.

Service. In Matthew 25:31–46, Jesus presents a challenge to his disciples to serve human needs in his name. The *Book of Order* offers a panoramic view of the Presbyterian understanding of mission that is consistent with Jesus' teaching (G-3.0300).[11]

One critically important phrase remains, modifying each of the six items of diversity: **"to suit culture and need."** Were this phrase to be left off, the impression might be that choices would be determined on the basis of taste or interest. God sends God's people into God's creation to tell God's good news in word and deed. This final reminder reaffirms the goal announced at the beginning of G-4.0401: to be **"responsive to diversity in both the church and the world."**

This paragraph clarifies that our response, if we are to be faithful to our Lord, must both **"suit"** the needs of persons and be offered in a way that recognizes the cultural dynamics that are crying out themselves for the good news. Because these cultural dynamics are so different, this is an invitation to celebrate diversity.

Openness—the focus of G-4.0402—seems intrusive in its placement between the two other paragraphs on diversity. Why do we switch topics at this point, turning to the issue of inclusiveness? The shift is from something external that can be readily monitored to an aspect of community that is felt at an emotional and spiritual level. Inclusiveness has to do with comfort level, with the sense of "being at home" in one's surroundings. Inclusiveness can be spread through hospitality.

An elderly Presbyterian carried pencil and paper with him to worship. He sat in different areas of the church each Sunday. If people he didn't know sat near him, he would introduce himself after church, visit a bit, and ask whether he and his wife might visit them that afternoon. He would write down their names and addresses so that he would remember them. This gentleman was busy in many enterprises, yet he was committed to making his church welcoming.

G-4.0402 describes the quality of life essential for an inviting fellowship of faith: "**Our unity in Christ enables and requires the church to be open to all persons and to the varieties of talents and gifts of God's people, including those who are in the communities of the arts and sciences.**"

This paragraph is composed of only one sentence. It reminds us that the theme of this chapter is "**Our unity in Christ**," without which there is neither church nor hope. Unity is Christ's gift to the church (G-4.0201). Refocusing on Christ as our unity excludes other often proposed possibilities, such as doctrinal uniformity, theological or liturgical consistency, or programmatic faithfulness. While these may reflect for some the unity Christ gives to the church, they do so only dimly. To elevate one or more of them to the level of operational requirement would be to deny Christ's gift. Maintaining the focus on unity as Christ's gift continues to be as challenging as it is imperative.

Christ's gift of unity has two definite implications, in that it "**enables and requires the church to be open. . . .**" Jesus Christ, as Lord of the church, both **enables and requires openness.** We sing and pray that the Lord help us in all our troubles. Touched by the Spirit of Christ, we are enabled to do more than we could have otherwise imagined. What remains is to choose to exercise what power we have received. The issue is whether and to what degree we will obey the Lord of the church.

To be faithful is "**to be open.**" As Jesus Christ willingly received sinners, tax collectors, lepers, the Samaritan woman at the well, and many others considered social and religious outcasts, so we too are called to that sort of openness. To be open is to be expectant, to stand on tiptoe, expecting opportunities and challenges where we can bear witness to our Lord and Savior. Our identity as those for whom Christ died and rose again makes it possible for us to open up to others in ways that transcend our natural abilities.

A crucial question here is: "Open to whom and to what?" The response given is breathtakingly expansive. Persons of faith are able to witness their faith to **"all persons"** only by the grace of Christ. This witness includes that expectant possibility of being able to say just the right word that will make a difference in the life of the next person one meets. The conviction that we are all created in the image of God means that every human being is a candidate for receiving our welcoming hospitality. The scope of such responsibility is suggested in Deuteronomy 26:12–15, where the faithful give a tithe of their produce to "the aliens, the orphans, and the widows" (Deut. 26:12), those who otherwise have no claim on the community. As a recent discussion of Colossians suggests, "The universal claim 'Christ is all and in all' is in the service not of violent marginalization but of redemptive inclusion."[12]

G-4.0402 continues, **"and to the varieties of talents and gifts of God's people. . . ."** Here, faith gets real, incarnate. Sometimes it is extremely difficult to deal with church members whose talents and gifts differ from what others consider usual or ordinary. The varieties of gifts about which Paul wrote in 1 Corinthians 12:4–10 can be surprising for those who have a particular idea in their minds about what it means to be a member of a specific church.

At the end of this section comes what many Presbyterians likely consider a curious phrase: **"including those who are in the communities of the arts and sciences."** It has been reported that during the drafting of the *Book of Order* prior to the 1983 reunion, one member of the drafting committee continually requested that such a phrase be included somewhere as a way of acknowledging the historic role Presbyterians had taken in these fields. Now the phrase stands to alert us to those who contribute creatively to our life together. The inclusion of W-2.2008, "Other Forms of Proclamation," is another evidence that the original plea was heard.

This paragraph (W-2.2008) elicited a request in 1990 that the General Assembly answer the question, "Is it permissible not to hire a person because of that person's religious preference?" The response proposed by the Advisory Committee on the Constitution and approved by the 202nd General Assembly noted that, while the Civil Rights Act of 1974 exempted religious corporations from its provisions, "unless a religious viewpoint directly impacts upon work performance, the church must be mindful that our unity in Christ enables and requires the church to be open to all persons" and cited G-4.0402.[13]

The final paragraph of this section (G-4.0403), the climax of this chapter, presents a challenge. Its particular provisions resulted from numerous actions and statements in both predecessor denominations, beginning in 1955.[14] The Confession of 1967 denounced "every form of discrimination," and concluded, "Congregations, individuals, or groups of Christians who exclude, dominate, or patronize their fellowmen, however subtly, resist the Spirit of God and bring contempt on the faith they profess."[15] Article 8 of the "Articles of Agreement," continues to remind us of concerns related to "Racial Ethnic Representation, Participation and Organizations" that emerged in the reunion of 1983.[16]

The text of G-4.0403 is:

> **The Presbyterian Church (U.S.A.) shall give full expression to the rich diversity within its membership and shall provide means which will assure a greater inclusiveness leading to wholeness in its emerging life.**
>
> **Persons of all racial ethnic groups, different ages, both sexes, various disabilities, diverse geographical areas, different theological positions consistent with the Reformed tradition, as well as different marital conditions (married, single, widowed, or divorced) shall be guaranteed full participation and access to representation in the decision making of the church (G-9.0104a).**

This provision begins with a declaration of intent: "**The Presbyterian Church (U.S.A.) shall . . .** " The Preface to the *Book of Order* tells us that SHALL and IS TO BE/ARE TO BE signify practice that is mandated." They are the most emphatic verb forms in the *Book of Order*, and they are repeated twice in this first sentence to emphasize two dimensions of our commitment to diversity.

The first call or challenge of G-4.0403 is that "**The Presbyterian Church (U.S.A) shall give full expression to the rich diversity within its membership.**" The phrase "**rich diversity**" may seem odd at this point, where emphasis on diversity has already been so present. These two words suggest that often within our existing membership gifts and talents that would enrich our fellowship are in abundance, were those members invited to share these assets with the community. This is a reminder to review our stewardship of the considerable human resources we have in our membership, the assets for mission that are sadly underutilized in our mission and witness. We need to wake up to the riches in our midst, rather than to lament the lack of other resources we think we need. We need to take seriously that, "Christ calls the Church into being, giving it all that is necessary for its mission to the world" (G-1.0100b).

The second call or challenge is more daunting: "**shall provide means which will assure a greater inclusiveness leading to wholeness in its emerging life.**" Even as we review what treasures we have, we also are called to "**provide means,**" that is, to figure out how to go about designing and implementing ways to "**assure a greater inclusiveness**" (G-4.0403), to expand the diameter of our circle of fellowship. We are called to implement in our daily life those declarations about inclusiveness in the previous paragraph of the *Book of Order*. In short, we are called to practice what we preach. G-5.0103 puts it bluntly and emphatically:

> The congregation shall welcome all persons who respond in trust and obedience to God's grace in Jesus Christ and desire to become part of the membership and ministry of his Church. No persons shall be denied membership because of race, ethnic origin, worldly condition, or any other reason not related to profession of faith. Each member must seek the grace of openness in extending the fellowship of Christ to all persons (G-9.0104). Failure to do so constitutes a rejection of Christ himself and causes a scandal to the gospel.

The crisp language of the first sentence in G-4.0403 concludes with the aim of full participation: "**leading to wholeness in its emerging life.**" This phrase reminds us of earlier passages in this chapter of the *Book of Order,* appreciating ways Presbyterians relate to the larger church (G-4.0100–.0200). The word **"wholeness"** reaches back to the Hebrew word, *shalom,* translated as both health and wholeness. We are called to move toward a community that in its life together witnesses to God's intent for all creation, a foretaste of God's ultimate plan for humanity.

This second call also reminds us that we have fallen short in our striving for such wholeness. Part of us wants to respond, "but we are doing as much as we can!" However, those words are also a confession of having fallen short. Even our defensiveness testifies to our lack.

An illustration of one attempt to respond to this challenge was the approved goal of the 208th General Assembly (1995): "increasing the racial ethnic membership to 10 percent of the Presbyterian Church (U.S.A.) membership by the year 2005, and to 20 percent by the year 2010."[17] Nine years later, the *Minutes* of the 216th General Assembly (2004) show that as of the end of 2002, the target percentage projected was 8.5%, while the actual percentage of racial ethnic members was 9.0%.[18] The question is, what will be the report to the 217th General Assembly in 2006?

This is not the major "**means**" available. The *Book of Order* includes a provision that, "each governing body above the session shall elect a committee on representation" (G-9.0105a). The responsibilities and composition of this committee are detailed in the paragraphs following the above statement. Creating this new feature of church life in 1983 was a way of ensuring that the commitment to inclusiveness in the *Book of Order* became more than words on a page.

The last sentence of G-4.0403 is long. The basic structure is: "**Persons . . . shall be guaranteed full participation and access to representation in the decision making of the church.**" The sentence ends with a reference to **G-9.0104a**. Before we consider the specified groups of persons, we need to understand what constitutes "**full participation and access to representation in the decision making of the church.**"

The focus is on who is able to make decisions in the church. While officers in governing bodies make operational decisions, *all* members are expected to participate fully in the life of their church. This includes voting in meetings of the congregation, being informed of issues before those issues are voted on, and serving when elected in the various entities of the church. One sign of danger in the spiritual life of a church is the shrinkage of the circle of those who make decisions.

"**Access to representation**" is the essence of this provision. In secular language, this means the right to vote, which includes access to the discussion prior to the vote. Most of us know that the right to vote often does not mean winning. It is the right to be heard, the opportunity to tell one's views on the subject under discussion. Still, it is the voting majority that determines the outcome (G-1.0400: "that a majority shall govern"). It is also true that a final decision is " . . . decided by the collected wisdom and united voice of the whole Church" (G-1.0400).

Now we turn to the categories of persons, those to whom the guarantee is promised. Each of the seven following is a kind of "protected category," which means that persons in each category are to be included on committees, commissions, and other entities of the Presbyterian Church (U.S.A.) beyond the local churches. These categories vary considerably in specificity, meaning that some of the groups are more readily discernable than others. While this listing was new in the 1983 *Book of Order,* concern about these issues had been evident for a long time. The General Assemblies of both predecessor denominations had taken actions in all these areas, to one degree or another. When the drafters consolidated these seven social issues in one list, the drafters summarized much of American Presbyterian history. Since 1983 these categories have continued to serve as important guideposts amid the significant demographic changes in our country as well as in our church.

All racial ethnic groups. American history demonstrates how "**racial ethnic groups**" have been considered "second class" persons to greater or lesser degrees throughout much of our history. The ideal of our Declaration of Independence, "that all men are created equal," was often denied by a majority view, which continues to ignore minorities to the present. The missionary enterprise of earlier times has engendered a "new immigration" as Presbyterians from other countries have come to the United States seeking to become part of the American Presbyterian community. Such additions to the *Book of Order* as G-12.0102k demonstrate a positive response to this new reality.

Different ages. Ageism is as old as Paul's counsel to Timothy, "Let no one despise your youth" (1 Tim. 4:12), which stands as a reminder that the tendency to discount persons because of their age is nothing new. In 1991 the 203rd General Assembly added some guidance for this general instruction: "'Different Age Groups'" are persons who are unlike each other by virtue of the different stages of life they represent, such as youth, adulthood, or old age. In order to assure greater inclusiveness in the church, participating persons from different age groups are needed. "The age groups and ages they contain are as follows: Youth - 25 and under; Young Adults - 26–35; Adults - 36–55; Senior Adults - 56 and up."[19]

Both sexes. In spite of the New Testament's prominent evidence of the role of women in the life of the early church, American Presbyterians were slow to recognize the importance of gender equality in church life. Historian James Smiley reports that gender issues began to demand major attention following World War II. In 1956 the PC(USA) decided to ordain women as ministers. The PCUS made that decision in 1964.[20] The positive results of this awakening to treasures in our midst are now generally appreciated, even as we lament that so many were ignored for so long.

Various disabilities. When the Americans for Disabilities Act was passed in 1990, this provision had been in the *Book of Order* for seventeen years. "Access" has more depth of meaning when we consider those with disabilities. The accounts of Jesus' healings in the gospels, such as Luke 5:17–26, remind us that such sensitivity is not limited to the present day.

Diverse geographical areas. More inclusive governing bodies are especially aware of the need to have the various regions they cover present for their meetings. People from different localities often bring unique experiences and perspectives to the work of the church.

Different theological positions consistent with the Reformed tradition. This dimension has some connection with the previous one, geography. Because theology matters to Presbyterians, we tend to take it so seriously that we allow the nuances to obscure the deeper convictions of faith. Indeed, what may seem nuances to one person are considered essential doctrine to others. Civility in ecclesiastical matters is essential if we are to be a faithful, covenanted community.

Different marital conditions (married, single, widowed, or divorced). This category was added to the *Book of Order* here and in five other places after the Council on Women and the Church and the Committee on Women's Concerns overtured the 197th General Assembly (1985). The overture lifted up the fact that "there are many nonordained persons in the employment of the Presbyterian Church (U.S.A.) who are single by choice, widowed, divorced, or divorced and remarried."[21] Since 1983 these categories have been particularly helpful to the ability of synods and General Assembly to demonstrate evidence of our Presbyterian commitment to inclusiveness.

G-4.0403 has become a lightning rod of sorts. Some ask: "Why should such social concerns clutter up our *Book of Order*?" My response is that these seven categories of diversity call for and activate social sensitivities that are too often missing in American life in the early years of the twenty-first century. Put another way, these "protected categories" provide an outline for civility.

God grant that we Presbyterians become a beacon of civility as a witness to our gracious Lord, Jesus Christ.

Notes

1. Samuel Wells, "Hearing God Out," *Christian Century*, vol. 122, no. 9 (May 2005): 9.
2. George Newlands, "Quisquilia Princetoniana," in *The Princeton Seminary Bulletin*, vol. XXVI, no. 1 (New Series: 2005): 5. This issue contains material presented as Dr. Iain R. Torrance was inaugurated and installed as the Sixth President of Princeton Theological Seminary. *InSpire* is a periodical published by Princeton Theological Seminary.
3. The Second Helvetic Confession, *The Book of Confessions*, 5.141.
4. A Brief Confession of Faith, *The Book of Confessions*, 10.4.
5. *Good News Bible: The Bible in Today's English Version*. (New York: Thomas Nelson Publishing, 1983).
6. While the origin of this motto is unknown, some attribute it to former president Charles Wishart, who defeated William Jennings Brian for moderator of the General Assembly (Presbyterian Church in the United States of America) in 1923 following the Scopes trial in Tennessee.
7. This orientation is presented in John Noel, "Darwinism, Religion, and Reconciliation," *The Journal of Presbyterian History*, vol. 82, no. 3 (Fall 2004): 169–179.
8. Setri Nyomi, "Living Faith in a Challenging Era," *The Princeton Seminary Bulletin*, vol. XXVI, no. 1 (New Series 2005):13.
9. Brian J. Walsh and Sylvia C. Keesmaat, *Colossians Remixed: Subverting the Empire* (Downers Grove, IL: InterVarsity Press, 2004), p. 7.
10. "Whole church" in this action of the General Assembly in 1797 from G-1.0400 refers to the majority of "a representation of the whole" indicated earlier in the deliverance.

11. See especially in G-3.0300c(3). William E. Chapman, *Mission Symphony: Notes for the Third Millennium* (Louisville: Witherspoon Press, 2004), provides reflections on the theological basis, as well as the implications of G-3.0000.

12. Brian J. Walsh and Sylvia C. Keesmaat, *Colossians Remixed* (Downers Grove, IL: InterVarsity Press, 2004), p. 113.

13. "Request 90-2. Concerning the Employment of Staff," *Minutes of the 202nd General Assembly (1990), Part I*, p. 254. Taken from the *Annotated Book of Order*, computer version. 2003–2004.

14. See footnote to this provision in the *Annotated Book of Order*, computer version, 2003–2004. "This section has no single source. See on various subjects: PCUS (1971, 170) Overture to replace exclusively masculine words; PCUSA (1955, 103) Overture F, representative nominating committee; UPCUSA (1963, 316) Overture D, color, origin, worldly condition; (1971, 308) Overture F, on offices, race, ethnic, sex, marital status; (1975, 96, 189, 538) Overture and report on inclusive language; (1975, 67, 299) Overture B, C, D, on fair representation, male, female, ages, ethnic; (1978, 64, 399) Overture L, men and women; (1979, 84, 531) Overture J on disability.

15. The Confession of 1967, *The Book of Confessions*, 9.44.

16. Appendix B to the *Book of Order*.

17. *Minutes of the 208th General Assembly (1996), Part I, Journal*, p. 378.

18. *Minutes of the 216th General Assembly (2004), Part I, Journal*, p. 681. The total racial/ethnic number (220,941) did not include an estimated 12,247 attending fellowships.

19. Overture 90-18, *Minutes of the 203rd General Assembly (1991), Part I, Journal*, p. 751.

20. James H. Smylie, *A Brief History of the Presbyterians* (Louisville: Geneva Press, 1996), p. 128.

21. *Minutes of the 191st General Assembly (1985), Part I, Journal*, pp. 144–145. (Item 30 in the *Annotated Book of Order*, 2004–2005.)

Afterword

⟞⟞⟞⟞

"A Season of Discernment: Report of the Task Force on Peace, Unity, and Purity" appeared on August 26, 2005, two weeks after I finished the draft of this book. Two questions increasingly had pressed on me as I worked on the final chapters: "How will my view of what I consider to be 'distinctively Presbyterian' compare with what the Joint Task Force produced?" and "Would the other books I have written become no longer relevant?"

Under the heading "Resources for Constructive Engagement: Presbyterian Polity" in the Task Force Report, we read that "Presbyterian polity is an expression of deep theological convictions."[1] Statements about Peace, Unity, and Purity follow. I deeply appreciated this sentence as a succinct and accurate summary of my own understanding of Presbyterian polity.

Turning to the dynamic of Presbyterian polity, the report continues:

> Historically, Presbyterian polity has been neither static nor singular. The denominational traditions that have formed the current PC(USA) placed different emphases on the particular dimensions of polity that they viewed as most distinctively "Presbyterian." Yet they all sought to maintain equilibrium between certain principles of governance that theologically distinguish Presbyterian church life and discipline from other Christian communions.[2]

The phrase "maintain equilibrium between certain principles of governance" again expresses in different terms the same dynamic I found in G-1.0300 and presented in my *History and Theology in the Book of Order: Blood on Every Page*.[3] I used the concept of paradox to suggest the persisting dilemmas outlined in

G-1.0300 and the need for continuing adjustment amid changing circumstances to maintain an appropriate balance.

Changing circumstances have continually affected Presbyterians in America in various ways. The eighteenth century featured the formation of governing bodies at each level, as well as a division and reconciliation. The nineteenth century was a time of growing pains as Presbyterians explored the implications of ministry to an expanding country and divided again, this time about how to relate church life to government.

The twentieth century was a time of reunions and separations. There were three reunions: with the Cumberland Presbyterian Church in 1906, the United Presbyterian Church of North America in 1958, and the Presbyterian Church in the United States in 1983. There were also separations: from the Orthodox Presbyterian Church in 1936, the Bible Presbyterian Church in 1938, the Evangelical Presbyterian Church in 1956 and 1981, and the Presbyterian Church in America in 1973.[4]

The General Assembly became the arena for resolving emerging imbalances. Two reports are especially noteworthy because of their impact on the life of the church. The first was the Special Commission of 1925 whose final report in 1927 stands as a major statement regarding issues about ordination as well as the respective roles of the more inclusive governing bodies.[5] Because of its wise analysis of the situation, it is often cited and thus continues to play a significant role in the life of the Presbyterian Church (U.S.A.).

The other report that I consider significant, though it is less familiar, is the Report of the Special Committee on the Los Angeles Presbytery Memorial in 1953. The question at hand concerned the role of presbytery regarding Presbyterian ministers working for other church bodies. Commenting on precious controversies and how seemingly unprepared the church was to deal with them, this Commission said that: "It has . . . quickly found that the problem had very deep roots and many serious complications. The solution sought and found has been a pragmatic one aimed at solving no more than the unavoidable issues involved in the specific case."[6] The result was an amendment to the *Book of Order* currently in G-11.0405b.

Whether "A Season of Discernment" will find its place with these two actions will be determined initially by the 217th

General Assembly meeting in June 2006 in Birmingham, Alabama. What is more certain is that Presbyterians will continue to wrestle with the principle expressed in 1788:

> That, while under the conviction of the above principle we think it necessary to make effectual provision that all who are admitted as teachers be sound in the faith, we also believe that there are truths and forms with respect to which men of good characters and principles may differ. And in all these we think it the duty both of private Christians and societies to exercise mutual forbearance toward each other. (G-1.0305)

Like so much else in our Christian faith, we are called to understand one another and to exemplify the grace of our Lord Jesus Christ.

Notes

1. "A Season of Discernment: The Final Report of the Task Force on Peace, Unity, and Purity of the Church," www.pcusa.org/peaceunitypurity/, line 769, p. 20.
2. Ibid., lines 785–789, p. 20.
3. (Louisville: Witherspoon Press), 1996.
4. James H. Smylie, *A Brief History of the Presbyterians* (Louisville: Geneva Press, 1996), p. 86.
5. *Minutes of the General Assembly, 1927*, pp. 56–86, Found under "Citations from Predecessor Churches" in *The Constitution of the Presbyterian Church (U.S.A.) Part II, Book of Order Annotated Edition* 2003–2004.
6. *Minutes of the General Assembly, 1953*, pages 110–133. Found "Citations from Predecessor Churches" in *The Constitution of the Presbyterian Church (U.S.A.), Part II, Book of Order Annotated Edition* 2003–2004.

Leader's Guide

Initial questions:

1. **How many sessions are you planning?** There are six chapters in the book, plus a brief "Afterword." This guide is divided into six sessions, one session for each book chapter. The introduction describes four basic concepts inherent in my view of what is distinctively Presbyterian. Chapters Three and Four discuss G-4.0300. Chapter Three may require more than one session, if you are working in one-hour sessions.

2. **What folks make up the group you will be leading?** Persons who are new to the Presbyterian tradition may need further explanation of terms and orientation to the role of the Book of Order in the official life of our church. Those who have been Presbyterians longer may find that some of the material differs from their understanding. In this situation, greater sensitivity and a slower pace are in order. Persons whose experience is limited to one geographical area may also find that their experience differs from those in another region.

Some additional materials that could help you:

1. Bible
2. Current *Book of Order* and current *Book of Confessions*
3. Current Presbyterian Planning Calendar for denominational information
4. Access to www.pcusa.org, the denominational Web site

Best wishes with the process of exploring this chapter of the *Book of Order* and considering with others the implications for your discipleship according to the Presbyterian way!

Introduction:
Four Presbyterian Characteristics: My Reflections

You may find the four concepts I propose as basic to the way Presbyterians are distinctive to be unnecessary, too challenging for the people in the group, or somewhere between these extremes. Your assessment should guide you in whether and how you will handle this material.

Step 1:

The objectives for the initial session might be to:

    a. Get acquainted
    b. Distribute books, if necessary
    c. Introduce in your own words the goal(s) for this study
    d. Begin to examine the issue of *Distinctively Presbyterian*

Step 2:

One way to begin to look at the issue in the book would be to ask each person to give an answer to: "What does it mean to be distinctively Presbyterian?" If you have access to Dirk Wierenga's book, identified at the beginning of the chapter, you might have persons read two or three of the personal profiles he gives or display some of the photographs. Another possibility would be to ask for brief descriptions of someone outside your congregation who a participant feels is "distinctively Presbyterian." A third way would be for each to share what it means to be "distinctively Presbyterian."

Step 3:

Present each of the four characteristics in order, ensuring that the group begins to comprehend how these emerge in church life. Use definitions and examples from the book or your experience to assist the group in understanding the implications of each concept.

    a. Dilemmas
    b. Dialogue
    c. Debate
    d. Deference

You may decide that there is another sequence in exploring these concepts. Clear understanding should facilitate the group process as the study continues. It may be useful to return periodically to these four concepts during the rest of the study.

Step 4:

Assign Chapter One as the reading for next week. Suggest that participants write their own definition of "church" before they do the reading, so that they might discern how their definition compared with what they found in Chapter One. You will be able to discuss this next week.

Chapter One: *The Church—Universal and Particular*

G-4.0100 presents the Presbyterian understanding of where and how our church is related to the universal church, the one to which we refer in the Apostles' Creed when we say, "I believe in the holy catholic Church." The progression is from the general to the specific.

Opening:

Welcome any new members of the group. Introduce new persons and have returning members give their names. Briefly summarize the first session.

Step 1: G-4.0101

Invite the group to examine G-4.0101, a definition of "Church universal." Some questions might be:

1. What is your reaction to this definition?
2. What word or words trouble you?
3. What questions does this definition raise?
4. What surprises or difficulties did you find in this definition?
5. Do you find this definition comforting or distressing?

Another approach would be to compare G-4.0101 with one of the hymns from nos. 411 to 444 in *The Presbyterian Hymnal*.

Step 2: G-4.0102

Note the word "reasonable."

1. What does this suggest about this step in the process?
2. Does the group find this reasonable? surprising?
3. What other reasons for "particular churches" are there?
4. Consider the phrase "local expression." Does this phrase complicate or simplify your understanding?
5. What are the implications of "therefore" for thinking about our church?

Step 3: G-4.0103

Prepare a sheet with G-4.0101 in one column and G-4.0103 in another. Provide time to look at the handout. Then ask the group how these two definitions are:

a. Similar?
b. Different?
c. Connected?

Step 4:

Discuss how these two definitions affect how we understand our local particular church. What are some of the consequences for members? For the church?

Step 5:

Assign reading Chapter Two of *Distinctively Presbyterian*, which deals with unity. Alert the group that they will find three understandings of unity discussed. They will also learn some Presbyterian history that may surprise them. Propose that each member come to the next session with one surprise or question arising from their reading.

Chapter Two: *The Unity of the Church*

The report of the Task Force on Peace, Unity, and Purity to the 217th General Assembly in 2006 leads into the latest formal discussion of unity. This topic surfaced in new ways in the twentieth century in terms of the growth of the ecumenical movement as well as strong controversies among Presbyterians. Leaders may want to download or otherwise obtain copies of the Task Force Report, and look at the Afterword in the D*istinctively Presbyterian*.

Step 1:

On three pieces of newsprint, write a different heading, one of these: "Unity in Mission," Unity as Oneness," and "Visible Unity," and have these displayed as the group arrives. Invite each person to write a comment or question from their reflection on their reading.

Step 2:

Taking the comments in order, use them to explore the meaning(s) of "unity" in the text of G-4.0200 as discussed in the Chapman book. Some questions that may help in this process are:

1. How does unity as gift affect our understanding of unity?
2. What do you think is the connection between unity and mission?
3. What are some "benefits of Christian community" others might consider worth sharing?

Discuss the adequacy and/or inadequacy of G-4.0402 as an understanding of Ephesians 4:5–6? (Bear in mind this is a dilemma as discussed in the Introduction.)

Step 3:

G-4.0203 might be compared with a differential equation as an indication of its complexity. Reconciliation, while not mentioned, lurks as a theological term for bringing diverse people together. Resistance is characterized as obscuring potential unity.

Explore with the group their questions and concerns about the affirmations in this provision, as well as the movements toward unity discussed in *Distinctively Presbyterian*.

Step 4:

Ask the group, "What might our church (and we as a group) do to reduce the obscurity of the unity of the church?"

Step 5:

Ask each member to read G-4.0301 and to write down **one or two** of these principles that intrigues them. After reading Chapter Three, "Nine Principles of Presbyterian Government," invite each participant to write down how initial reactions have changed.

Chapter Three: *Nine Principles of Presbyterian Government*

In preparation for this step, prepare four cards with each of the four characteristics of Presbyterians in the Introduction (dilemmas, dialogue, debate, deference) for display in the room. Depending on the group, dealing with each of the nine "principles" of Presbyterian government may well take more than one group session.

Step 1:

Invite the group members to share their results from the assignment. Suggest that if a principle is presented that others have also identified, conversation on that principle continue until all have offered their reactions. This step may need to be continued into another session.

Step 2:

Make sure all nine of the principles are covered. Explore why those that did not emerge in Step 1 were left out.

Step 3:

Remind the group of the four characteristics from the Introduction. Explore with the group how the four characteristics and the nine principles are related. **Note:** Should the discussion of Chapter Three extend into an additional session, you might consider announcing the assignment in Step 4 for the next session as well.

Step 4:

Assign Chapter Four, "Declaratory Principles." Explain that these three principles are longer. Provide the context in which the nine principles of G-4.0301 operate.

Chapter Four: *Declaratory Principles*

A major change in tone and focus occurs between G-4.0301 and the three remaining principles, the topic of which is also "principles." Chapman's book recognizes this by starting a new chapter, dealing with G-4.0302—.0304. These are still important principles, even though a sharp shift in style and presentation occurs.

Step 1:

Suggest that the group compare G-4.0302 with G-4.0101, and G-4.0201. What is the difference? How does sharing affect the nature of the church's unity?

Step 2:

G-4.0303 presents a dilemma (Introduction). Have the class explore what is necessary to sustain both "sides" of the dilemma of inclusiveness. How would this affect how our church goes about its mission? Its worship?

Step 3:

How does G-4.0304 relate to G-4.0100? What does the group think would be the effect of this sentence, were more Presbyterians to become aware of it?

Step 4:

Ask the group to read Chapter Five, "Mix and Match." Continue to consider the four characteristics of Presbyterians while you consider where our church is in terms of the two categories discussed in the chapter.

Chapter Five: *Mix and Match*

This should be the final session for your study. The two concepts, "diversity" and "inclusiveness," often trigger strong emotional reactions.

Step 1:

Begin with a discussion of diversity. Clarify that diversity here relates to sociology, so the focus is on diversity of people and what diverse groups bring with them. Watch for an opportunity to suggest that the call for diversity implies change.

Step 2:

Ask which of the six areas of corporate life in our church would likely be most resistant to change:

- Form
- Practice
- Language
- Program
- Nurture
- Service

Step 3:

G-4.0402 adds another layer of challenge: "inclusiveness." How welcoming is our church to visitors? Do we tend to be more welcoming to some than to others? Are the twin "goals" of inclusiveness and diversity a dilemma? How then does a church begin to fulfill the dual challenge? (See how this leads into the Step 4.)

Step 4:

G-4.0403 appears to resolve the dilemma of the preceding two provisions by calling for "a greater inclusiveness leading to wholeness in its emerging life." Engage the group in considering how your church might begin to move toward such a goal.

Step 5:

Are there some "next steps" they are ready to take, as a result of the study?

Step 6:

Thank the participants for their involvement in the study.

Note from the author: I am interested in how this Leader's Guide functions. Kindly send your comments and suggestions to: polywonk@aol.com.